Responsible Adults

Responsible Adults

in the

Church School Program

BY IRENE SMITH CALDWELL

Published for

THE CO-OPERATIVE PUBLICATION ASSOCIATION

THE WARNER PRESS :: ANDERSON, INDIANA

268·434

(12)

149224

Foreword

That adults be dynamic, growing, and responsible is increasingly important in our age. The period of effective influence and service in the average life of man has practically doubled in the last generation alone. A veritable "new continent" of rich resources for leadership has been discovered in this increased life expectancy. In 1900 the life expectancy in the United States was some forty-eight years. It is now seventy. This is an increase of twenty-two years, and every prediction is that the trend will continue.[1]

The span of adult life is lengthening. And whether we are thinking of young adults, middle adults, or this new continent of older adults, we are forced to recognize the fact that the decisions and attitudes of adults determine the direction in which society will move. Adults form a more significant influence on children and youth than any other generation. This fact speaks loudly to responsible adults of the church today. It says that the church must challenge and guide all adults to a quality of spiritual and ethical living, not only for their own sakes, but also for the sake of their influence on children and youth.

Adult education has, therefore, become a real frontier in Christian education. If the church can help parents to be growing personalities, and if the teachers and leaders of the church and community can find in every experience a challenge to dynamic growth and can develop an open, searching attitude toward life

---

[1]Lawrence C. Little, Editor, *Charting the Future Course of Christian Adult Education in America,* The University of Pittsburgh Press, Pittsburgh, 1959.

and truth, then we can expect the same to be true of those whom they lead.

In light, then, of the importance of adulthood, we should examine all phases of the church's educational program for adults, especially as expressed in the life of the local congregation. The purpose of this book is to provide the responsible adults of a local congregation with a guide to an experience of actually testing and rebuilding their adult educational program. Let the group approach the experience with prayer, but with devout urgency, knowing that adults hold the key to the present as well as to the future, both in society and in the church. Whether today's as well as tomorrow's adults find in life a constant challenge to dynamic spiritual growth may be determined by the church's program now.

The author wishes to dedicate this book to "The Questers," a group of young adults who are earnestly striving to become a fellowship of growing Christians.

Irene Smith Caldwell

Portland, Oregon

Contents

Our "age" is determined more by our interests than by our years

1   What Adults Can Be!

A famous woman has been called "the surrey with the fringe on top," for she has outlived her generation but not her regal charm or her wide usefulness. Although she is seventy-five years old, she has a growing concern for world needs and shows a vital interest in every great cause. She says that she may look as old as Methuselah but she never feels old, for every period of her life has had its own challenge to dynamic growth and responsibility.

"Rubbish" is the name the modern artist Hoffman has given to his picture of a dejected, discouraged man of middle life.[1] This man, dressed in his business suit, crouches on an old box beside two ash cans, his unfolded newspaper near by. Dimly, in the background one can discern the towers of the city—symbols of wealth, competition, industry, mechanization. Yesterday, he stood up and said, "I am a person. I will make a difference in this world of business." But today the sense of responsibility is gone. It may never come back. He may settle for the routine, the ordinary, and the defeated.

The changing culture of our world requires of adults a power to maintain a vigorous idealism and, at the same time, a practical ability to deal with reality. The Christian faith holds that such power is available through Jesus Christ who said, "I came that they may have life, and have it abundantly" (John 10:10, RSV). Those who receive him are to have "power to become children of God" (John 1:12, RSV). And through the presence of the Holy Spirit man may receive power to witness and to live victoriously regardless of changing cultures and circumstances. (See Acts 1:1-8.) Such a faith holds that adults may meet every period of life as a challenge to grow into larger, more responsible, and more victorious persons.

Responsible Adulthood

Adults have the potential capacity for great growth and continuous learning. This realization requires a new sensitivity to man's search for the meaning of life as it relates to him. He often gropes blindly and even sinfully to satisfy this search for the purpose of his existence. He may even give up the search and settle for the static, the ordinary, and the defeated, as was so vividly pictured by Hoffman. Herein lies a vital challenge to the church. Can the spirit of the adult program of the church be such as to keep man alert to his own destiny? How can the church so meet man's need as to help him become a dynamic victorious person?

To Be a Person

To be a dynamic, growing person in our problem-conscious world requires a new understanding of "person." The term is used here to describe man as God intended him to be. Such a person knows that he is created by God to live in harmony with Him and his universe. He feels that he is in some measure fulfilling the destiny for which he was created. He is not free from the problems of his world, but he is able to use these problems for his own growth. He seeks to find himself and his place in a world of widening relationships and new factors in the culture. These factors threaten him, but they also present to him unequaled challenges and opportunities for personal growth.

Very threatening to the selfhood of adults is the constant pounding which tends to break individual initiative and make *conformists* of us all. "Hidden persuaders" are very real, and they may drive adults toward material luxuries as a substitute for higher values. The desire for status may easily replace the desire for inner growth.

Human values may be easily obscured through *automation,* which displaces the skill of man by very clever machines. The threat is not only an economic one; it is also a challenge to man's feeling of worth. If a machine can do man's work more efficiently than he, what sense of vocation can he find? Closely related to automation is an ever-increasing *mobility.* About one fifth of the population move every year. The lack of rootage, together with the loss of former supports for moral and ethical standards, face adults with new decisions and temptations.

Strangely, as the world becomes "one world" of jet travel, mass communication, and outer space, many adults tend to tighten themselves into narrow, prejudiced, provincialists. Fear impedes the development of world-mindedness in circumstances where negative attitudes of superiority and prejudice cause conflict. In addition, this realization of a larger world tends to accentuate man's sense of smallness and insignificance. In a big world like this, where does man count? He feels alone and very much afraid. In his search for himself it is not strange that anxiety and a sense of meaninglessness may at times overtake him.

Such is our world. Yet this is the environment in which personhood must develop. What does it mean to be a dynamic person in this kind of world?

Steady, patient growth in freedom. To grow in freedom may be the adult's most difficult task. Conformity to the demands of others undermines courage. The growing person struggles to remain a free, deciding individual. He refuses to let the persuaders of life or the demands or criticisms of others embitter his life or determine his goals. While he learns to accept his physical needs and limitations and to admit the circumstances, he also determines to find and fulfill the purposes for which he was created.

An ever-enlarging sense of belonging. Adults continue to need the sense of belonging, although the relationship will take a different pattern from that of childhood. The adult, too, needs to feel that he belongs, not for what he can contribute but because as a person he is sacred and significant. He is in a world which tends to by-pass persons in order to use them for financial or status ends. As one wag said, "Why, I have friends I haven't even used yet." When the social order, whether in the name of friendship, business, or even religion, exploits man, he becomes defensive and anxious and feels lost and apart. Honest acceptance is necessary if one is to have this feeling of belonging. Man must feel needed and wanted, not for what he can do, but for who he is. Because he needs so much to be accepted, any sense of being rejected becomes a devastating and hindering experience.

The sense of belonging develops in a spiral fashion. First, one belongs to his family; but soon, without belonging any less to his family, he belongs to his social group, his church, his community, his nation, and his world. Without denying any of these groups, he may come to a sense of belonging to all that is, has been, and ever will be. Then, in reality, he has become a person in belongingness.

Active and honest involvement with other persons. To be the person God intended him to be, one must love as well as be loved. He must accept as well as receive acceptance. Such involvement brings deep hurt as well as great joy. To care deeply often means to suffer deeply. Persons who are afraid to care are in danger of losing their personhood. Nowhere is this truth better expressed than in the words of Jesus when he said, "Truly, truly, I say to you, unless a grain of wheat falls into the earth and dies, it remains alone; but if it dies, it bears much fruit. He who loves his life loses it, and he who hates his life in this world will keep it for eternal life" (John 12:24-25, RSV).

Yet in our society man often endeavors to keep his caring on a "safe" plane. He keeps his relationships shallow lest he himself be hurt. He feels it is naïve to be greatly moved because of a blighted life or a suffering world. But to be a person means everdeepening and ever-widening involvement in the struggles of others.

A growing demand to understand life and its deeper meanings. The dynamic person hungers and thirsts to feel that life makes sense. He cannot be satisfied to know what happens; he wants to know why it happens and to see a cause-and-effect relationship. He stands with his mind wide open for new understanding of reality. However, this does not mean that he grasps every new wind of doctrine; rather he tests and tries the new, and when he finds it more authentic than that which he formerly held, he earnestly measures his life by the deeper value. He is not willing to settle for certainty, but lets a spirit of search be a mark of his spirit. He searches for a meaningful unity between God, man, the world and all that is, and he feels himself a part of this harmonious unity.

A growing desire to co-operate in creativity. The dynamic person wants to play a role in bringing redemption to mankind. He wants to feel that he has given his best that others may have the more abundant life. He is not niggardly with himself, but wants to know that mankind is blessed by his having lived. Deep inside him, he groans to make his creative contribution, whether it be a new type of seed to feed mankind, a cure for cancer to prolong man's life, a poem to inspire, a sermon to challenge, or a cathedral to uplift. But man knows that he cannot be creative alone. Indeed, he depends on many others and most of all upon his Creator. He is most dynamic as a person when he loses himself in working together with others and with God in creativity.

Experience of relatedness to God. The dynamic person acts as a balanced whole; that is, he is a harmonious personality, with his inner feelings and attitudes and his outer conduct fitting into one pattern. But this personhood cannot be fastened on a man like the ornaments on a Christmas tree. It is more like the fruit of a tree, which finds nourishment from inside and develops first the bud, then the blossom, then the full ripe fruit. This harmony of personality cannot be separated from harmony with the very nature and origin of man's being, for man is created by God and can never find his real self until he finds harmony with his Creator. When man opens himself to God and honestly seeks to live in harmony with God's purposes, God through the Holy Spirit brings such harmony and power. The church's part is to provide the climate for spiritual growth and response; then each adult as a deciding, active being must, himself, work out his own answer. We believe that every adult desires to be, and can be, a dynamic person when he realizes his relatedness to God and to all mankind.

In dealing with dynamic personhood, certain needs have been pointed up. Since physical needs are always evident, these received only a passing mention. The six needs which have been emphasized are: the need to grow in freedom, the need for a sense of belonging, the need to become involved with other persons, the need to understand life's deeper meanings, the need to co-operate in creativity, and the need to experience relatedness to God. How dynamic the person has become is determined by how well these needs are being fulfilled.

In speaking of the growth of adults the Overstreets have put it this way:

> How large, in mental and emotional terms, is the adult: the forty-year-old; the sixty-year-old? That depends. If *growing up* has meant for him chiefly *settling down*, he may, even in his middle years, be shrinking in psychological stature. . . . His "size" will depend, as it has ever since he was born, on whether or not he is growing out toward his environment. It will depend on whether he is still pioneering with his distinctively human faculties: still moving beyond the known into the unknown; still putting himself, voluntarily, into a position to be surprised, caught off guard by new aspects of reality, humbled by his own ignorance, stretched by new insight.[2]

The question which boldly stares us in the face is: How can the adult church school so meet these needs, that adults will grow and become those dynamic persons who live by spiritual values.

To Be an Adult

"Now that I am a man, I am done with childish ways,"[3] Paul testified. Yet for most persons this is not as easy as it may sound. When we say that Grant Johnson is an adult, we refer to the fact that he is now physically mature; he has crossed the line from youth. Perhaps he is able to vote and to support himself financially. He may participate in the adult church school. Yet in a very significant sense he may not be an adult, for adulthood is an achievement rather than a point in time. As a matter of fact, no human being ever fully reaches adulthood in this sense.

There are "struggles of the soul" in the path to true maturity, with certain tasks more pertinent to specific periods. Robert J. Havighurst has given the name "developmental tasks" to such struggles. He defines a developmental task as "a task which arises out of a certain period in the life of an individual, successful achievement of which leads to his happiness and to success with later tasks, while failure leads to unhappiness in the individual, disapproval by the society, and difficulty with later tasks."[4] If one is making progress in the achievement of adulthood, he will meet successfully the tasks of his particular period in life.

Growth in early adulthood. Early adulthood, the period between eighteen and thirty, is full of rich opportunities for growth, yet often results in arid selfishness. During adolescence the person has struggled for freedom from his ties to family; now he must form new ties of his own and himself carry the responsibility for maintaining them on a mature level. The danger is that after suffering through the tie-cutting experience, he will fail to form new ties and escape into a terrifying loneliness. "Early adulthood is the most individualistic period of life and the loneliest one, in the sense that the individual, or, at the most, two individuals, must proceed with a minimum of social attention and assistance to tackle the most important tasks of life."[5] Or if he does form new ties, he may seek those where he can shift major responsibility to others, thus forming his new ties on a childish level and failing to mature.

Space here will permit only a brief mention of the most significant of the tasks of early adulthood.

1. *Forming a mature relationship with a marriage partner.* This idea includes the selection of a mate and the ability to assume emotional responsibility in the relationship.

2. *Becoming a parent.* This is normally a major crisis in life, and provides great opportunity for maturing and growth.[6]

3. *Getting started in a vocation.* The young adult must find

and prepare for a vocation which is both emotionally satisfying and economically supporting.

4. *Accepting social responsibility.* Each adult must find his place to make his rightful contribution to the society of which he is a part. Often the young adult seems too busy with getting everything possible for himself to carry his share of responsibility for others.

5. *Finding a profound faith.* The faith and religious affiliations of the young adult can no longer be dictated by his parents. He must find and take responsibility for his own relationship with God and with the church. Perhaps the most subtle threat of all is that he will settle for form, church attendance, and being religious rather than find the propelling strength of a divine relationship which reaches into every other relationship.

These tasks of young adulthood may be summarized as forming mature identifications and assuming mature responsibilities. They face every young adult and challenge him to dynamic growth. The way in which he meets the challenge, and is thus prepared to accept later tasks, is dependent on the quality of his earlier emotional relationships and the support and guidance provided through his present relationships.

Growth in middle adulthood. Those years between concentration on preparation and the years of retirement are considered the middle years, at whatever age this occurs. Roughly, the period covers from age thirty to about sixty-five. This is the period of man's greatest contribution and of society's greatest expectation. These may be the "creative years" or they may be the years when the spirit goes dry. How one meets his tasks will determine which it will be.

Briefly stated, the chief tasks of middle adulthood are:

1. *Adjusting the dream to the reality.* The acceptance of one's limitations and the confines of society without losing his idealism is one of the difficult tasks of the middle years. For one to accept

the fact that there are some things he may never accomplish, and yet to keep working with zeal, takes courage. To realize that his contribution will be rather ordinary, and that his children may be just average, and still give his very best is a task of this period.

2. *Managing economic pressures.* This is the time of highest economic expectancy and demand. The pressures of the American standard of living place strong temptations on middle adulthood. To maintain a satisfactory economic standard of living without doing so at the cost of higher values is a real problem for this age.

3. *Accepting physical changes.* For both men and women this age brings certain physical changes and limitations. At a time when life's demands are highest, the middle adult is faced with a decline in physical capacity. Each one must adjust his way of living to these changes and find ways of higher productivity with less physical effort.

4. *Handling psychological changes.* Here again, at the time when parents most need stable emotions because their children are in the throes of adolescence, parents often find that they cannot understand themselves and their emotions. While it is difficult for a home to withstand "two generations of adolescents at the same time," a sound way of handling these psychological changes must be found.

5. *Freeing adolescents emotionally.* Just as one of the tasks of adolescence is to become free from parents, so a task of parenthood is to release youth, and still maintain a sense of purpose in life.

6. *Relating to the spouse as a person.* Maturing love requires that the husband and wife find great emotional satisfaction in each other. During the child-bearing, child-rearing period the role of parent may have veiled the role of husband and wife, but once again this relationship is dominant.

7. *Preparing for later maturity.* Psychological preparation for later maturity is probably more significant than economic preparation, although the latter is important. During middle life adults must develop new interests and abilities appropriate to declining strength.

8. *Finding the meaning of life.* The really significant task of middle adulthood, and one that permeates the treatment of all other tasks, is that of developing a mature view of life and the universe. We often refer to this as a man's "philosophy of life." He will find it necessary to rethink such questions as: What are the values by which choices will be weighed? Will choices be made in the light of material gain, or will decisions be based on personal relationships with others and with God?

Whether or not these years are creative years depends to a large extent on the attitude which the adult brings to them. If his dominating purpose is to gain security, he draws within himself and becomes a tight little self-protected ball. But if his purpose is to spend himself, he accepts the risks of investing in others. Then these years become years of growth and creativity.

Growth in later adulthood. At retirement, whether that be at sixty-five or later, man's chances are better today than ever that he will live at least another ten years. And he will still have new experiences ahead of him and new situations to meet.

Sherrill has pointed up that the central problem of later adulthood is simplification. He describes it as "achieving simplification of life in the physical, material, and spiritual aspects, so that the soul may with less and less impediment progress toward its chosen destiny."[7]

The older adult is like the mountain climber who, having struggled with all his might, finally reaches the peak and then murmurs, "Now if I can only get down alive." His task is to come down from status and prestige gracefully, and yet to remain emotionally alive. This "coming down" experience forms itself into certain tasks which may provide the opportunity for continuous learning.

1. *Accepting simplification of status.* To be sure the older adult is still the parent of his children, but his role has changed. People formerly spoke of John Evans and his son, Robert; but now they speak of Robert Evans and his father. The focus of importance in family relations is now on the son rather than on the father. To accept this changing role without losing one's sense of worth becomes a real test of maturity.

2. *Adjusting to decreasing physical strength and health.* Decreasing strength and health brings increasing dependence. To persons who have taken pride in their independence, this increasing dependence is hard to master. In trying to be kind, society may become overly protective and, in providing physical care, fail to recognize the need for self-sufficiency and initiative.

3. *Finding new avenues to usefulness.* In America one's job is the center of usefulness for most men and women. When he must retire, man faces the task of making his existence meaningful. Even if psychological preparation has been made earlier, he often finds the reality empty and futile. To find a way to carry out his stewardship and thus feel needed is necessary but difficult.

4. *Viewing material things in their diminishing value.* Most older adults must adjust to a lower economic income and change habits accordingly. If along with reduced income there is also a sense of dependency, this may be a severe test of the character structure of old age. However, if the income is provided in such a way as to allow the preservation of self-respect, the reduction does not prove too severe a threat. For emotionally mature adults, there is a devaluating of *things* as life nears the end. They measure their wealth, not by the number of things they have, but by the fewness of their wants. They come to value

personal relationships and opportunities for service far above the accumulation of things.

5. *Growing in the spiritual sphere*. The true hope for growth in later adulthood is in the spiritual sphere. Here, there is no need to think of coming down, for there is the opportunity of reaching higher than ever. Indeed, this spiritual triumph may come as a result of the physical and emotional suffering of these years. Through his past and present suffering one may come to see spiritual values and leave "a parting gift to life which surpasses in value all that he has ever wrought before."[8]

6. *Preparing for and facing death*. Perhaps this is the primary task of the later years. In early adulthood, man has been looking forward to life. In the middle years, he is in the midst of life. Now he finds a simplification, a kind of sorting out of those things which are eternal. If he has met these tasks well, life on this earth prepares him for death, which comes to mean not death, but life in transition.

Such as these are the needs, the problems, and the opportunities for growth which confront adults today. Is it too much to expect that through the church adults may find power to live all of life as dynamic, growing persons?

For Group Planning

1. The first task of responsible adults in the church will be to take an objective look at the present organized adult activities of the specific congregation. Each adult organization should be asked to fill out some such blank as Chart I in the appendix of this book. In a group planning session the results of these reports should be shown on a large chart with name, purpose, program, study materials, and membership of all adult groups. This understanding of the present program would be the first step toward evaluation.

2. Now let the adults of the church face the questions raised

in this chapter as objectively as possible. As they look at the large chart of all adult organizations, let them consider the six basic needs with such questions as follows:

a) *The need to grow in freedom.* What are some real threats to personal freedom in our society? How does the church sometimes thwart man's freedom? Is the spirit of these groups such that they encourage growth in freedom? How well are we meeting this need?

b) *The need to belong.* What percentage of the adults belong actively to some group in the church? Does their participation indicate a significant emotional feeling of belonging? What percentage take responsibility for activities of the group? Do members show interest in each other outside the group? Do the groups have high-prestige and low-prestige members? Are there persons who feel rejected by some groups? Are there cliques? How well do we help every adult meet the need to belong?

c) *The need to become involved with other persons.* Do the members show personal concern for each other in times of illness or need? Do they reach out sacrificially to others who are unfortunate? Do the groups provide concrete ways for each member to invest himself in the burdens of the world? How well do we help adults express deep concern for others?

d) *The need to understand life's deeper meanings.* Are the studies deep enough to challenge the adults' best thinking? Are the discussions of eternal significance? Do they relate to present problems and needs? Do people say what is expected, or do they answer honestly? Do the programs bring response in changed lives? How do we evaluate our church as a school in understanding life's deeper meanings?

e) *The need to co-operate in creativity.* How many adults have regular opportunities to serve in creative ways? Is the opportunity fitted to their interests and abilities? Is the service of eternal significance? Do we challenge to service without providing opportunities for service? Do we provide adequate training for service? In addition to money and attendance, what specific service does each member give?

f) *The need to experience relatedness to God.* Through what specific means does the adult church school help persons to a vital relationship with God? Is the worship related to the lives of the members? Does the school help adults to a maturing understanding of God? Do the adults through the school find power for victorious Christian living? Are the members developing an ever-deepening sense of stewardship and dedication?

3. Some real effort at evaluating whether groups are meeting needs is essential. Chart II of the appendix should be used in each group in the church. The results will be considered carefully both by the groups and by the adults making this study. Chapter 5 outlines positive ways of developing suitable group climate.

4. Another part of the evaluation will relate to the tasks of the three periods of adulthood. As you look at the large chart on which are recorded the results of the present adult organizations, you may divide the class into three groups. Let the groups check the tasks listed in this chapter under early adulthood, middle adulthood, and later adulthood. The question to be faced is: How well does the adult program of our church help the adult meet his specific tasks at each period?

FOR FURTHER STUDY

Clemmons, Robert S., *Dynamics of Christian Adult Education*, Nashville: Abingdon Press, 1958, chap. 10. 143 pp.

Ernsberger, David J., *A Philosophy of Adult Christian Education*, Philadelphia: Westminster Press, 1959, chaps. 1 and 2. 172 pp.

Havighurst, Robert J., *Developmental Tasks and Education*, New York: Longmans, Green and Company, Inc., 1952, chaps. 6, 7, 8. 100 pp.

Howe, Reuel L., *The Creative Years,* Greenwich, Conn.; The Seabury Press, 1958, chaps. 2, 3, 9, 10. 239 pp.

Knowles, Malcolm S., *Informal Adult Education,* New York: Association Press, 1950, chaps. 1 and 2. 272 pp.

Lentz, Richard E., *Making the Adult Class Vital,* St. Louis, Mo.: Bethany Press, 1954, chaps. 7, 8, 9. 112 pp.

McKinley, John, *Creative Methods for Adult Classes,* St. Louis, Mo.: Bethany Press, 1960, chap. 1. 96 pp.

Sherrill, Lewis J., *The Struggle of the Soul,* New York: The Macmillan Company, 1952, chaps. 1, 4, 5, 6. 155 pp.

Zeigler, Earl F., *Christian Education of Adults,* Philadelphia: Westminster Press, 1958, chaps. 1, 2, 3. 142 pp.

---

[1] Albert Bailey, *Art and Character,* The Abingdon Press.

[2] Harry and Bonaro Overstreet, *The Mind Goes Forth,* W. W. Norton and Company, p. 95.

[3] The Bible: A New Translation by James Moffatt. Copyright 1922, 1935, and 1950 by Harper & Brothers. Used by permission. I Cor. 13:11b.

[4] Robert J. Havighurst, *Developmental Tasks and Education,* Longmans, Green and Company, p. 2.

[5] *Ibid.,* p. 72.

[6] Some adults, either by choice or because of circumstances, may not marry or have children. Nevertheless they have the task of assuming adult responsibility and of finding a satisfactory adjustment to their particular situation.

[7] Lewis Sherrill, *The Struggle of the Soul,* Macmillan, p. 130.

[8] *Ibid.,* p. 136.

DO | DON'T

We learn by doing—if we are allowed to do

2 Adults Can Learn

The foundation on which the adult program will be built is the firm belief that adults can learn if they accept the responsibility for their own growth and development. Havighurst holds that, of all the periods of life, adulthood is the fullest of teachable moments. He defines a teachable moment: "When the body is ripe, and society requires, and the self is ready to achieve a certain task, the teachable moment has come."[1] For instance, one of the very teachable moments for adults is at the birth of a new baby. At this time parents often feel both a new sense of responsibility and an awful inadequacy. They desire to be the best parents possible and are reaching out for help. Any crisis or climax in life, of which there are many, produces a teachable moment. Yet adults often fumble through and come out defeated, less able to meet the next crisis.

Havighurst says also that adulthood is the emptiest of efforts to teach. The church must become aware of the fact that adults have the capacity for continuous learning. The adult program shall take note of the vast amount of teachable moments.

The folklore that "you can't teach an old dog new tricks" and "I'm too old to change" simply is not true. "Extensive studies by means of intelligence tests show that mental ability grows rapidly during adolescence, reaches a peak during the late teens and early twenties, and then gradually declines at the rate of about 1 per cent each year after forty years of age. More recent experiments involving actual learning situations reveal, however, that it is not the *capacity* to learn that declines, but the *rate* of learning. They merely learn a little more slowly. And there is good reason to believe that even this slowing-up process is due in large part to lack of practice. Those adults who engage in learning activities throughout life seem to lose very little of their intellectual efficiency."[2]

Indeed, adults must learn, for it is impossible to teach a youth of twenty how to meet the problems of a man of fifty. Each can learn best when his teachable moment comes. Adults have certain advantages in learning, particularly in those types of learning which require a backlog of experience and which deal with relationships and a mature sense of values. Since a significant role of the church is to help man grow in relationships and to clarify values, it would appear that adult education is particularly pertinent to the church.

Adult Learning Means Maturing

When we think of adult learning we are not thinking primarily of amassing facts or developing skills. Rather, we are thinking of personality growth and the ability to judge issues by mature values. Dr. Harry Overstreet describes adult learning thus: "The business of man is to mature psychologically as well as physically, to mature along lines which are unique in him and what he healthily shares with all his fellows, and to continue this maturing process throughout his life."[3]

But growth in maturity is often painful and always slow. One cartoonist put at the top of his sheet, "There is nothing so painful as a new idea," and at the bottom, "I hope this gives you pain." Since new ideas may be painful, adults tend to settle down into habitual ways of thinking, feeling, and acting. They resist change because of the disturbance and struggle; but disturbance and struggle must be dealt with if there is to be any meaningful learning.

Adult Learning Is Personal

In order for an adult to learn most effectively, he must recognize a personal reason for learning about a given topic. It is not enough that his leader, or the national committee, sees the subject as an area of need for adults; he himself must see the personal reason. He no longer thinks of himself as preparing for life; he is in the business of life, and he needs help for life now. He feels within himself a lack or tension, and he struggles to find the answer or to meet the situation well. This tension may arise from life experience and his own sense of inadequacy, or it may come from his encounter with some teaching of the Christian gospel related to his personal life.

Sometimes an adult resists that which would bring tension. One person jokingly put it, "My mind is made up; don't confuse me with the facts." In such a case the protective wall needs to be broken through, so that the person will feel the tension and come to recognize his need. For this reason, adult learners should become involved in the choice of study topics and must share the responsibility for the success of the learning experience.

Sound criteria for evaluating propsed adult study courses are: (1) the choice of study materials is based on needs of the group; (2) time spent on a subject is governed by needs father than by dates; (3) adults have a choice in selection of materials; (4) the members accept responsibility for the success of the venture; (5) the aims of a study are clearly related to life needs.

Climate for Learning

Just as two seeds dropped into the soil in distant lands produce plants of a different size because of the climate, so ideas may be stunted or may flourish because of group climate. For successful learning, certain conditions are necessary.

Freedom of expression. "I've never mentioned this to anyone but," and "I may be considered a heretic but" are phrases that indicate the ice is breaking and adults are becoming involved in learning. Many adults sit as silent members in the discussion. Some of this reticence may be habit or lethargy. Yet, a surprising number of adults wish desperately to explore their ideas and problems, but they are afraid to bring them up. Others speak, but they give the expected answers, never daring to depart from the concepts they feel the church holds. Some repeat pious phrases and religious jargon which they do not mean and they do not really understand.

If adult learning is to take place, real communication is essential. We must overcome the fear we have of each other and of the leader, regardless of his educational attainment. Developing a climate where people are not afraid to show their inner feelings and where there is freedom of expression is one of our first tasks if we would have effective adult learning.

Responsible participation. Adults need to learn how to use freedom of expression as members of a responsible team. Given freedom, we may use it to argue in order to gain attention to the self, or we can express our hostility by sharp words or tactless barbs. More than one exploring teacher has found himself forced back into the "safe" lecture by arguments and tensions which arose because the group had not learned to use freedom well. Yet freedom is necessary and adults can learn to use it. Such learning requires a leader who thinks of himself in the role of guide. He, too, is honest in his purpose and in his need to learn. Yet he remains the leader and sees that the group is making progress toward a goal. Each member must willingly and fearlessly help in every way he sees open to him if the venture is to be successful. All honest contributions will be respected, but not necessarily accepted. There is freedom to question an idea, even if the leader presented it. Too much docile acceptance indicates either boredom or fear. Sometimes it becomes easier to agree than to think, but real learning is always growth toward independent thinking.

In the long pull toward responsible participation let us not be discouraged, for here most adults have a great deal to unlearn. They have been lectured and talked down to most of their lives. Often the effort has been to "cover the lesson" with little time for listening. Some weak efforts at participation have been ignored or dealt an authoritarian blow. Many adults may not know how to use this new freedom. Some may sit in silent fear, while others may run away with the opportunity. Maybe they have not learned to think. A discouraged leader put it this way: "Five per cent of the class think, 10 per cent think they think, and the rest would rather die than think." But let us not forget that adults are what they have been taught to be. Some groups have used a simple check chart to help adults understand their own participation. The following is a sample of such a check chart.

MY DISCUSSION BEHAVIOR FOR ONE MONTH

	1st	2nd	3rd	4th
I'm friendly and natural.	( )	( )	( )	( )
I'm open-minded.	( )	( )	( )	( )
I listen to the other person.	( )	( )	( )	( )
I hear the other person out.	( )	( )	( )	( )
I speak up.	( )	( )	( )	( )
I cite my experiences briefly.	( )	( )	( )	( )
I keep calm.	( )	( )	( )	( )

I stay in the group.	( )	( )	( )	( )
I ask questions.	( )	( )	( )	( )
I stay on the main track.	( )	( )	( )	( )
I think before I speak.	( )	( )	( )	( )
I study the material.	( )	( )	( )	( )

Here again, steady constant growth in freedom is a hard lesson, but it is well worth the effort.

A feeling of warmth. How each person feels about himself in the group determines whether it will be easy or hard for him to use the experience as a means to Christian growth. If he likes the leader and feels that the leader likes him, he will be more open for learning. If he feels wanted and needed and knows that people like him, he will be responsible. People learn more rapidly when they feel a spirit of warmth and concern.

Even the room conditions can contribute to this feeling of warmth and informality. Adult rooms should be homelike and informal. The learners should sit facing each other and the leader. The circle or round table seems best for adults.

Learning seldom takes place in situations where people are stiff and cold. Adults sometimes sit quietly or in light little whispering cliques; they may wish they were elsewhere. Some may even feel rejected, and no man can stand to feel rejected for long. Usually people do not intend to cause others to feel rejected. They may even be seeking security in their friends because of their own fear.

Persons quickly feel neglected if the following conditions prevail: (1) some members seem more important than others; (2) there is an "in" group which hangs together; (3) some are ignored; (4) people do not listen to all ideas; (5) the "in" group talks about good times they have had.

But there can be a feeling of "we-ness" in a group, which is conducive to learning. Then each member feels that he is accepted as a person in his own right. The members like each other and enjoy being together. Warm cordiality and informality make learning easier.

A sense of search. In this friendly, informal environment people are earnestly pursuing significant ideas. There is a sense of dealing with that which is vital. Humor may well relieve the tension at times, but there is no spirit of levity. While growth comes from feeling oneself a real member of a group, this in itself will never substitute for the confrontation of new truths. As these truths are explored and shared they challenge each learner to find a way to make them operative in his life. Leader and learners share together in a daring and perhaps even threatening search for truth.

When we think of adult learning, we are thinking first of that maturing experience which may come as the result of handling well life's problems, and second of growth in understanding which comes through a shared search for truth. It is the privileged task of the adult church school to supply the guidance and the climate for this, the only true learning.

For Group Planning

1. The group will want to take a look at study materials. They can determine what materials are being used in each group from the use of Chart I. Chart II will tell how the members feel about the materials. They may judge their use of materials by the criteria given in this chapter under Adult Learning Is Personal.

2. The adults should desire to set up some program for improving learning climate. They will need to make a careful evaluation of the results of Chart II. They may wish to make a flow chart of class participation. An observer should be appointed, without class members knowing that they are being observed. He would chart the class and draw a line from each person who speaks to the one addressed. The diagram might look something like one of these:

Diagram of Class Participation

Does class participation look like this?

TEACHER

Or does class participation look like this?

TEACHER

In order to observe the quality of the participation, Chart III could be used.

3. The church may want to set up a workshop in which leaders can experiment with and experience some group techniques.

FOR FURTHER STUDY

Caldwell, Irene S., *Adults Learn and Like It*, Anderson, Ind.: Warner Press, 1955, chaps. 1, 3, 4, 5. 112 pp.

Douglass, Paul F., *The Group Workshop Way in the Church*, New York: Association Press, 1956. 174 pp.

Havighurst, Robert J., *Developmental Tasks and Education*, New York: Longmans, Green and Company, Inc., 1952, chap. 1. 100 pp.

Kelley, Earl C., *The Workshop Way of Learning*, New York: Harper and Brothers, 1951. 169 pp.

Knowles, Malcolm S., *Informal Adult Education*, New York: Association Press, 1950, chaps. 1 and 3. 272 pp.

Lentz, Richard E., *Making the Adult Class Vital*, St. Louis, Mo.: Bethany Press, 1954, chaps. 1 and 2. 112 pp.

Lindhorst, Frank A., *Teaching Adults*, Nashville: Abingdon Press, 1951, chaps. 1, 2, 3, 10. 160 pp.

Little, Sara, *Learning Together in the Christian Fellowship*, Richmond, Va.: John Knox Press, 1956, chaps. 2, 3, 4. 144 pp.

Maves, Paul B., *Understanding Ourselves As Adults*, Nashville: Abingdon Press, 1959, chaps. 1, 7. 217 pp.

---

[1] Robert J. Havighurst, *Developmental Tasks and Education*, Longmans, Green and Company, p. 5.

[2] Malcolm S. Knowles, *Informal Adult Education*, Association Press, p. 17.

[3] Harry A. Overstreet, *The Mature Mind*, W. W. Norton, p. 41.

Too much of even a good thing can cause the loss of appetite for it

3   Growth Through a Balanced Program

A Balanced Program

We gladly recognize that adulthood is essentially an attitude rather than an age and that maturity is an achievement. We believe that persons and their needs must take priority over program and organization. But we come now to some very practical considerations. How can we plan a program for adults in the church school which will challenge them to continuous growth and dynamic Christian living.

It is a known fact that many adults do not turn to the church as a possible source of help when they face their deepest needs. Some of them complain that when they are wrestling with threatening defeat and fear, the church school is concentrating on theological debate and ancient history. Adults live at the "growing edge" of life, and the church must serve where issues are being met and decided. This requires a balanced program of at least six elements: worship, study, fellowship, recreation, stewardship, and evangelism.

Worship—the search to know God. Man's greatest need is for a meaningful relationship with God. This he finds principally through worship; therefore, worship must become central in the program for adults. If we think of the purpose of the church school as being to help people become growing, vital Christians, then there is no more important part of the program than worship. Worship needs to be experienced on several levels. A comprehensive program provides needed guidance on every level.

1. *Man needs personal worship* where through daily meditation, prayer, Bible reading, and the use of devotional literature he stands alone before God and comes into fellowship with him.

2. *He also needs family worship* where those who love each other most, both young and old, share in a common quest for God and come to feel his presence and his Lordship in their home. True family worship is a climate as well as an experience relating God to all of life.

3. *Man needs a small, intimate fellowship group* in which earnest seekers after God find spiritual renewal through praying and sharing experiences in an informal way. Such groups may come together at places of business, at factories, in schools, and in the home. Man is finding spiritual power through such groups.

4. *He needs the strength of a larger, informal worship* such as is possible in the church school. Here he may lead others in worship as well as be led by them. Since the informality and shared leadership of this experience is important, many churches are finding individual class worship more valuable than department worship. Each group meets in the classroom and, after a short period of fellowship, has a meditative kind of worship led by one of the members.

5. *Man also needs large group worship* where God is lifted up in majesty and purity. Here we speak of the whole church at

worship celebrating God's presence with most worthy music and highest thought. Through such worship, man sees life in its relationship to the eternal God and to his fellow man.

6. *Man needs to reach beyond his local church to wider horizons.* He is lifted higher as he worships with other Christians of his own fellowship and even beyond. He needs to know that strength which comes from feeling himself a part of a "great cloud of witnesses" lifting praise and worship to God. Such an experience may come through wholehearted participation in the World Day of Prayer, in community Festivals of Faith, or in great national or world conferences. Once man is swept out of himself in the power of such an experience, he can seldom be puny and narrow again.

Above all other elements, the church must be a worshiping group. Worship is central in the adult program of Christian education, for unless men worship they cannot grow as Christians.

Study—the search to know the truth. Man is in search for truth as it affects life—first his own life and then all of life. In the church school this search is for eternal truth and values. The Christian has the moral obligation not only to be intelligent in the field of religion, but also to measure his life decisions by eternal values. The real function of this search for truth is to help the learner meet and deal well with every situation he faces. This *truth that functions* must be a growing possession of every Christian.

Since certain "tasks" are to be met before others can be handled (as was discussed in Chapter 1), it is important that the adult study groups have an opportunity to express some choice of subjects for study. The Uniform Lessons, which cover the same general sections of the Bible every six years, need supplementing in order for the Adult Bible class to relate itself to the "tasks" of the various ages. It is true that this Bible-centered series treats the narrative portions of the Bible quite well, but it does not afford a wide enough range of study for meeting many of today's situations.

The use of some electives could afford a life curriculum to cover all areas of religious knowledge as well as personal needs. This plan uses some such device as an interest indicator to discover the interests and needs of the group. The interest indicator should be developed within the group. On it a number of possible topics for study will be listed and the members will check their choices. Chart IV in the appendix is to be considered only as a sample of such an indicator. A master plan requiring certain courses should be made, covering areas of study including Bible and beliefs as well as personal problems. Otherwise classes may concentrate on personal problems without acquaintance with the Bible, the source for dealing with such problems.

When the interest indicator has been checked by every adult to be included in the program of study, a committee will need to make an outline of courses and assign studies to specific groups. They will search for the best study books available on each subject. The study plan might look something like the outline on page 40. Each church would make its own chart according to the interest indicator and the study groups needed in that church. It may well be that some study groups will include all ages of adults, and others will be divided according to interest rather than by age.

However, the learning opportunities of adults should not be limited to these scheduled groups. The church will plan for special needs to be met through a series of forums, special classes, and workshops. The citizens' forum, the marriage clinic, the leadership laboratory, the music workshop, the institute on international relations, and the schools in Christian living are all illustrations of this type of program. These special activities are very fruitful, especially when outside leadership is used to bring new insights and breadth to the thinking of the group.

PLAN OF STUDY

COURSE OF STUDY FOR YOUNG ADULTS

TIME OF MEETING	COURSE	TEXT MATERIAL	LEADER
Sunday church school	My Christian Beliefs*	*Your God Is Too Small*—Phillips	Mr. Clayborne
Parents' Club 4th Friday	Building a Christian Home	*The Home Christian*—Kardatzke	Mrs. Morton
Weekly study group	Daily Decisions	*The Common Ventures of Life*—Trueblood	Mrs. Johnson

COURSE OF STUDY FOR MIDDLE ADULTS

Sunday church school	Being Growing Christians	*The Creative Years*—Howe	Mr. Simpson
Weekly study group	Understanding Adolescents	*Living with Teeners*—Overton	Prof. Mills
Bible class	Life and Work of Paul*	*A Man of Tarsus*—Phillips	Pastor

COURSE OF STUDY FOR OLDER ADULTS

Sunday church school	Personal Worship	*Discipline and Discovery*—Day	Mr. Gray
Weekly study group	Meeting Life Now	*Creative Old Age*—DeGruchy	Pastor
Bible class	Message of the Prophets*	*Ask the Prophets*—Knopf	Prof. Smith

*Indicates a required course.

The elective plan is meeting wide acceptance. It varies among the church groups, and adult leaders should work with their national board of Christian education in setting up the plan. Older adults, once resistance to change is overcome, often have the most exciting study of any adult group.

A comprehensive program includes adequate provision for members to make progress in their search to know the truth—and the truth cannot be compartmentalized into religious and secular truth. All truth is God's truth, whether it gives man a basis for conducting himself on the job and in his home, or tells him how to worship in the church.

Fellowship—the search to know others. The saying "you can't be human alone" is truer than appears at first sight. A normal, growing Christian life cannot be lived alone. Man needs the challenge of other "fellows in the same ship." Nothing molds personality like feeling oneself a part of a meaningful group.

In our day, a new emphasis is being placed on the church as the "redemptive community." Westphal has said, "This fellowship that is the distinctive and unique mark of the Christian church means living with one another, loving one another, forgiving each other, suffering for and serving one another, until we become so much a part of one another that our fellowship becomes one of the most precious things in the world and against anything that would violate that fellowship we set ourselves like flint."[1]

It becomes apparent that by fellowship we mean far more than surface relationships, although pleasant. This fellowship goes beyond human relationships and includes fellowship with God through Jesus Christ. True Christian fellowship is considered such a vital part of the adult program that Chapter 6 of this book is given to an effort to understand conditions for aiding the development of such a fellowship.

Recreational and social life—the effort to lose oneself. Today adults need the release from tensions which comes through interesting and engaging play. They need hearty laughs, wholesome fun, and diverting recreation to lighten the load of responsibility which bears heavily upon them. The church has long felt the need for recreation for youth, but it has failed to realize that adult needs for recreation may be even greater because of greater responsibility. The renewed interest in life, the robust health, the mental relaxation, and the moral discrimination which come from wholesome recreation are the right of every adult, and add tremendous zest to life.

Some have even dared to hold that many church difficulties would never develop if adults had regular opportunities to find relief from the tensions and strains of life in hearty recreation. Recreation that re-creates has no other purpose than pure fun. It is not used for building attendance, although such will surely result. There should be no sense of duty or skill requirement. Recreation is suited to the church if by it men and women find relaxation and come back to life with more emotional abundance and strength.

Stewardship—the effort to serve. In this big, dangerous, sinful world man longs to get hold somewhere and do his part to help his fellow men. Yet many adults live out their days in a sort of selfish desperation, knowing that the lives of men will not be very different because they have lived. The adult program of the church ought to provide a corner for each person to get hold and lift. Stewardship requires that a man invest his utmost for others, both through personal effort and the giving of his earnings.

We do well to see two kinds of service. One consists of those services which make possible the church as a functioning congregation. This "inside" service and giving returns to us in opportunities for worship and fellowship and in guidance for our families and friends. Here would be included such things as teaching, singing, sponsoring clubs, serving on committees, and taking care of the building and grounds. Adults cannot mature unless each one has the opportunity to carry his rightful share of responsibility in this group to which he belongs.

There is also "outside" service, where one goes beyond his own group to help those from whom he can receive no direct return. This most significant growth comes in enlarged vision and broadened sympathies when one reaches out to those who are in need from other communities, nations, and races. This type of service would include missionary enterprises, both at home and abroad. It would include the feeding of the hungry in disaster and famine areas, and, even more, helping the underprivileged to become able to help themselves. In order to help wisely, adults will take their social responsibilities seriously. It is not enough to feed a hungry man. Adults must work for social conditions under which the vast burden of human misery becomes unnecessary.

Evangelism—the effort to win others. Happily the church has come to recognize the validity of educational evangelism in which the adult church school has a powerful potential. At times we think of evangelism in the broader sense of confronting persons with the gospel and guiding them in their daily response to it. At other times we think of evangelism in its more direct sense of winning persons to a personal experience of Jesus Christ as their Savior and leading them to a discipleship with him. In both types of evangelism the adult church school has responsibility. It must ever be reaching new people with the good news of salvation. But it cannot be satisfied with an initial experience; it must challenge each adult to an ever-deepening relationship and a more mature service to God.

The task is large enough to include the talents of all adults. It is only because the church has lacked imagination and enlistment skill that nearly 80 per cent of adults in the church seem to have no place to do their lifting.

Chart V in the appendix may be used in checking the comprehensiveness of the church program for adults.

The Program Is Inclusive

Suppose the responsible adults of your church try an experiment. Figure in round numbers the adults for whom the church should be responsible. Then face this question: How many of these adults are now actively participating in even one of the six elements of the program except an occasional hour of worship? From your earlier study you have a list of adult organizations and the names of members in each. It might be well to check a list of all adults in the church, recording after each person's name the groups in which he actively participates. It is not enough that a church provide a balanced program; the realistic purpose must be to provide a balanced program for each adult. The idea of inclusiveness means that every adult is an active member of some study and fellowship group.

Since adults are independent, they will participate only in those activities which seem to meet some basic needs. Sometimes as they become adults they feel they have outgrown the Sunday church school. Some say that they do not care for Sunday school. Some just become careless and "sleep in" on Sunday morning, occasionally dropping in for worship. Why should young adults, at the very time they are beginning their homes and taking their place of leadership in the community, be called the "lost generation" to the church? It is a regretful fact that in many churches the majority of the adults do not actively share in the ongoing program. Why?

Well, consider Joan and Jerry, a couple who have been married four years. Both Joan and Jerry have been active in church from childhood. They both participated in the Youth Fellowship, and each has taught Sunday school. In fact, they met in their church college. But after they were married they didn't enjoy the youth

class quite so much. The lessons didn't seem to fit their lives, and
the young people seemed immature. The "young adult" class
now had members who were forty years old, and Joan and Jerry
didn't feel a part of that group either. Consequently, they
dropped church school and attend worship less and less
regularly.

Or consider Jim and Margaret Gray. They are in their early
fifties; this past June their last daughter was married. While the
children were at home, Jim and Margaret were a part of all the
church school activities for their children's sake. But now, since
they don't seem to belong in the Homebuilders Class and neither
are they retired, they never go to the Sunday school class or
family night activities any more. Jim is still on the church board,
but he and Margaret often go to visit their children on Sunday
now and leave church out entirely.

Then there are Joyce and Phil Patrick. They, too, have gone
to Sunday school from childhood. Phil was president of the
state youth fellowship. They met at an interracial work camp
while they were in college. Phil is a YMCA secretary and Joyce
is active in the P.T.A. They are greatly interested in the work
of the church. They go to Sunday school out of a sense of loyalty;
but how they long for a dynamic discussion group where there
is honest and mature searching.

All three cases, and they can be multiplied by the thousands,
point up one fact: Many people feel that the church school is
not meeting their need.

One Hundred Per Cent Participation

A genuine concern for the success of God's will through his
church expresses itself through active service. Therefore the
adult program of the church should push toward the goal of
100 per cent participation in the church's program. This means

that every adult will have some clearly named responsibility which he is to carry to insure the success of the venture.

The load of responsibility in the church is often carried by too few, too heavily burdened adults, while others long for purpose in their lives. The church has a stewardship of personal resources. It is not good stewardship to hinder the abundant life of some by overresponsibility, or of others by no responsibility. Some may not see their talents as useful to the church. Others may have experienced failure from lack of preparation. Deep down all surely crave to be useful for God.

The challenge to the church is to develop insight into all the various talents that may be used in the church, to develop a program of training, and to set up a personal enlistment program. This program will have within it many of the elements of the apprentice idea. A more experienced person will work with the less experienced until the latter has developed enough security and ability to carry the work alone. Talent scouts and interest finders may be helpful here, but nothing takes the place of a personal interview with each adult. A typical interview follows:

Mr. P. (Interviewer). Mrs. Macy, how do you feel about our church?

Mrs. M. It means very much to me, Mr. Porter—especially since my husband died. I just couldn't do without it.

Mr. P. Are there ways that it could mean more to you?

Mrs. M. Well, I like the worship very much. But sometimes I wish we'd sing more of the older songs.

Mr. P. I know how you feel, and I'll take your suggestion to the music committee. Do you ever feel that you'd like to do more for the church?

Mrs. M. Well, yes—but what can I do? I can't sing or teach, and now I haven't much money.

Mr. P. Mrs. Macy, what are some of the things you have enjoyed doing most in your life?

Mrs. M. There are so many things I used to do. I like to read poetry, and I have even tried to write some. I enjoy my flower garden and I love to cook, though I don't cook much since I am alone.

Mr. P. You would be perfect for a home visitor, Mrs. Macy. We have a number of people who are shut in. They need company and someone to read to them. Sometimes you could share your flowers or your cooking with them. They need someone like you very much.

Of course the definite plans will need to be carried through; but the church will have another worker, the shut-ins will be visited, and Mrs. Macy will be so busy and happy that she may forget her complaints.

All interviews will be different, but they are really not much more difficult than this one. Think what rich rewards and interesting experiences result from putting all these talents to work for God! The church needs the talent, and the adults grow spiritually through service. If imagination is alive, there is room for every talent somewhere in the church's work. These stand waiting to be enlisted and used.

One reason so many Christians remain immature and lopsided is that they have never felt really needed. They believe there is nothing for them to do but to listen and to give their money. They do not enter wholeheartedly into the total program, but take part in perhaps only one activity of the church, such as public worship. Of this we may be certain: If the adult is to experience full and balanced Christian growth, he must engage in worship; he must give himself in service; he must continue learning; he must experience deep Christian fellowship; and he must reach out that others too many know the Christian life.

For Group Planning

1. The adults of the church school will want to look at the comprehensiveness and balance of their program in relation to this study. Copies of Chart V in the appendix could be carefully filled out by the group. A committee should study the results and bring recommendations regarding the weak areas. Or perhaps the adults would divide into six committees to make a study of each of the elements as carried out in the local church. The committee on worship would bring suggestions for ways to improve worship. The committee on study would survey the curriculum materials and make recommendations accordingly. By this means a self-analysis of the total program would be made along with a suggested program of improvement.

2. Make a list of all the adults related to the church. Beside each name list the activities in which the person takes part. A study of such a list will picture gaps in providing a program for every need. Also it will show persons who do not find for themselves a balanced program in the church. It will be well that responsible adults seriously ask why.

3. Beside each name on the list of adults list the definite responsibilities held by each person. Consider whether some are overburdened while others have no responsibility. If your stewardship of personnel resources seems to be poor, a program should be set up looking toward 100 per cent participation.

FOR FURTHER STUDY

Clemmons, Robert S., *Dynamics of Christian Adult Education,* Nashville: Abingdon Press, 1958, chaps. 3 and 4. 143 pp.

Ernsberger, David J., *A Philosophy of Adult Christian Education,* Philadelphia: Westminster Press, 1959, chaps. 3, 4, 5. 172 pp.

Lentz, Richard E., *Making the Adult Class Vital,* St. Louis, Mo.: Bethany Press, 1954, chaps. 4 and 5. 112 pp.

McKinley, John, *Creative Methods for Adult Classes,* St. Louis, Mo.: Bethany Press, 1960, chap. 2. 96 pp.

Zeigler, Earl F., *Christian Education of Adults,* Philadelphia: Westminster Press, 1958, chaps. 3 and 4. 142 pp.

---

[1]Edward P. Westphal, *The Church's Opportunity in Adult Education,* copyright 1941. The Westminster Press, p. 76. Used by permission.

DO   **DON'T**

Together we can accomplish many things

4   Sound Working Principles

Interesting adults! They resist organization, yet they demand efficient functioning. They are "joiners" and individualists at the same time. If a function doesn't seem to meet a need, they kill it by staying away. They want a say about their program, but they are sometimes unwilling to take responsibility for their decisions. They want to stay in the same class all their lives.

It is the purpose of this chapter to point the direction of sound working principles for these "interesting" adults in their relation to the adult church school.

How Is It in Your Church?

When we speak of the adult church school we are thinking of all those activities for adults which use the educational approach primarily. Each church will need to decide what activities shall be considered a part of the adult education program. Usually this includes such groups as the Sunday church school, adult interest groups, Bible classes, parents' clubs, women's auxiliary or missionary society, men's work, and hobby and recreation groups for adults.

In some churches each of these groups tries to operate a full and balanced program of worship, study, recreation, and service, seemingly unaware that other groups claim some of the loyalties of the very same members. Not only is there overlooking and overlapping, but sometimes even rivalry and competition creep into the relationship.

Now this will not be considered strange when we remember that each organization sprang up to meet a very definite need at the time. A great deal of effort is necessary to keep a group developing, and in the praiseworthy zeal for one group, another worthy group may become neglected.

In few instances have responsible adults sat down together and, on the basis of the needs of the adults, developed a complete and comprehensive program. Rather, most churches have several groups attempting to minister to the needs of all who will attend. How is it in your church?

A Sound Plan of Organization

Of this we are certain. Each church must move as rapidly as possible from a lot of fragmentary efforts to one inclusive and comprehensive adult program. Such a program requires *organization*. By organization we merely mean setting up the ground rules by which people can work together efficiently to get a job done. The rules are always secondary to the job, but they are necessary. They are to be simple and flexible, yet clearly understood and carefully obeyed.

A sound plan of organization would call for a council or committee on adult work. If the church is small, the board of Christain education may serve as such a committee with one or two of its members designated to represent the adult program and to carry out decisions as they relate to adults. Let us not forget that adults in the small church have the same needs as adults in the large church. The small church simply calls for more ingenuity in program in order to meet the needs of all.

How would a council on adult work be formed, and what are its main functions?

The Council on Adult Work

The council should be composed of at least one representative from each adult organization in the church. Some groups are divided in such a way that they need more members in order to be fully represented. Sometimes representation may cut across groups to special needs. Usually there are representatives from the following groups: the adult Sunday church school, each of the three age levels of adults, men's work, and women's work. This would make six members besides, of course, the pastor and the minister of Christian education or chairman of the board of Christian education. Many churches will have representation from the home department, the family life committee, and other active adult groups. Each church will look at its own adults and decide who should be on the council in order adequately to co-ordinate and build a sound program for ministering to all adults.

The council will need a chairman who will act as an adult director for the church. He will act not only as chairman of the council, but also as administrator to see that council decisions are carried out. Usually the chairman is chosen by the board of Christian education and is a member of that board. He should be willing to prepare himself to lead the council on adult work in building a co-ordinated, comprehensive, and ever-improving program for adults.

Grouping Adults

While adults enjoy being in groups, they are individualistic enough to want to have some say about the group to which they belong. Often this is upsetting to age-group-conscious administrators. For children, administrators have set up classes with regular promotions and found that children usually welcome the promotion. Then they set up adult groups with age limits and are dismayed when adults are unwilling to leave the younger group for the older one. If the program is inflexible, adults may even drop out rather than be forced into the older group.

At first glance such an attitude may seem to indicate that the adult is not willing to accept his age. There are plenty of jokes (with a barb behind them) about "life begins," "the golden age," and "the best is yet ahead." But greater insight will reveal sound reasons why even mature adults may not be happy with rigid conformity in adult grouping.

1. Adults have left the age-grouping period. Their friends are chosen more according to developmental tasks than according to age. The number of years married, the age of the children, and the vocation are far more significant here than age.

2. Adults like the security of a permanent group. A person can really give himself to a group if he feels he will be a part of the group all the rest of his life. He does not fear that one day soon after his thirty-fifth, or fiftieth, or whatever birthday, he will no longer be welcome in his group. Children have security in that they have group promotions.

3. Adults have needs to be met. If the purpose of the church school is to meet needs, then adults should be in the group where they feel their needs will be most nearly met.

Practically, there are three principal ways of grouping adults, with a number of possible combinations even within the same church.

Traditional grouping. The traditional plan is age and sex grouping. Here the groups may be large, with perhaps one men's Bible class and one or two women's classes. The method used is usually

mostly lecture, and the material is Bible content. Since there are
needs of adults that cannot be fully met by such classes, even the
traditional groupings now have variations. Often there is a
younger class of men and women below forty or forty-five, a
men's Bible class, and a women's Bible class. Another pattern is
to have age grading, but have men and women together in all
classes. In this case the divisions most commonly used are:

3 Groups	4 Groups	5 Groups
Married	Married	Married
or 25-40	or 21-30	or 21-30
41-65	31-45	31-40
65-	46-65	41-50
	65-	51-65
		65-

Even this pattern is becoming more flexible, trying to keep husband and wife in the same group and giving some freedom of
choice.

The traditional plan has some advantages. It can handle larger
groups, and does not require so many leaders. Since the lecture
is usually the method used, the sanctuary is a suitable place for
meeting. An active men's class with a lecturer of repute sometimes appeals to men who cannot otherwise be interested. But
it has the greater disadvantage of neither really meeting people's
personal needs nor providing for them the sustaining fellowship
which seems so desperately needed in our times.

Interest grouping. The idea behind interest grouping is that
a number of studies will be offered concurrently, and adults will
enroll in those classes which seem best to meet their interests
and needs. The period of study may be six months. A list of
courses is offered and leaders and pupils are enlisted. Groups
remain intact during the study and then re-enroll for the next
period. This plan has the advantage of being prepared specifically

with a certain need in mind. It provides an opportunity for closer acquaintance with many adults. It makes use of specialized leadership and materials. Yet it seems to lack in continuity and in providing a sustaining fellowship. Adults tend to drop out if there is no offering which fits their fancy, and they may not be re-enlisted. Eventually about the same group and teacher stay together regardless of the subject studied. The plan has been very successful in some churches, but it requires leadership and detailed planning. Usually, it is used only in the Sunday church school, and adults find their fellowship needs met in other groups.

Some churches find that a combination of the traditional class and the interest plan meets their need. They set up the regular age group classes, but also offer special interest classes. Any member may leave his regular class to join the special class at any time he feels the offering meets his need. One church had a special class for parents of preschool children, followed by a class for parents of elementary school children, later by one for parents of adolescents. Another church had courses such as Making Our Worship Meaningful, Being Christian in My Vocation, and Deeper Prayer Life. The possibilities are as wide as adult needs.

Fellowship grouping. The plan here is to consider both age and the related developmental tasks when first forming a group; then, once the group has been formed, it remains relatively stable. New persons will, of course, join the group if they seem to belong there by age and interest. A class name is selected which will be suitable at all stages of development, and the group, as well as the members, becomes one year older each year. Usually the studies are chosen according to interest and need, with members taking much responsibility for the success of the group. The fellowship goes beyond a study group and endeavors to affect every facet of life. Since the plan seems to have such great potential and yet requires understanding leadership, Chapter 5 of this book will be devoted to a clearer understanding of how fellowships are formed.

To the question, How many adult groups should we have? there is only one answer. We need to provide as many groups as are necessary to give guidance and fellowship to the largest possible number of adults. The church needs more ingenuity as to when and where such groups meet. Such groups are not limited to the church school hour, nor even to the church building. The "where two or three are gathered in my name" (Matt. 18:20) could be during lunch hour in a factory, or for coffee in a neighborhood, or even in a nursing home.

The Home Department

A fruitful but often neglected area of adult work is the ministry to the homebound. An ever-enlarging group of adults in our society are finding it impossible to go to the church building for their spiritual strength. The development of a home department is based on the idea that if people cannot come to the church, the church must find a way to go to them with the Christian message and challenge. The home department will minister to the following groups: those who are confined to their homes because of illness; the aged, either at home or in institutions; those who are confined in order to care for the aged or the ill; those who are prevented from attending the church because of their work.

The home department will need a director and a home visitor for each ten members. The department will provide material for discussion and inspiration, and it will keep each member in close touch with the activities of the church. The visitors will make regularly scheduled visits, with study and worship a significant part of each visit. Such work is exceptionally rewarding, but it requires careful planning and deep concern.

The home department will also plan for regular group meetings for adults who are institutionalized. Here is a place of real service for retired adults who are still active.

Encouraging Trends in Adult Work

Adult work in the church is coming into its own. Certain trends indicate the direction program planning, organization, and even church buildings are taking. The listing of such trends should be helpful to responsible adults as they plan for the future.

1. Those who will participate in an activity have a part in determining the type of activity.

2. To the extent that group members decide on the activity, they are responsible for the outcome.

3. Groups are guided in frequent self-evaluations.

4. There is more informality and flexibility in adult groups than formerly.

5. More adult groups are required, hence more leadership and classrooms. Adult rooms are informal and homelike.

6. Most classes prefer one unified experience of worship and study with some opportunity for social experience. The trend is to have informal worship in the classroom, rather than departmental worship.

7. The ever-enlarging older population requires a broadened program for older adults. They need opportunities for service and fellowship as well as study and worship.

8. Adults are eager to take more responsibility for visitation and community service.

9. The council on adult work acts to co-ordinate all adult activities.

10. The adult program is being broadened to include social and recreational activities, interest groups, retreats, and adult camping.

11. Both men's work and women's work are providing a broader and more worth-while program. They are undergirding the total church through study and intelligent participation.

12. There is a renewed emphasis on the Christian home and parent education.

13. There is a determination to take the church where people are.

For Group Planning

1. Your planning will be directed toward study of the organization of your adult department. Do you have a clearly defined organization for adults? Do you have a council on adult work? Does it represent every adult group? Could the work of the council be improved?

2. Make a careful study of the grouping of your adults. Consider the three plans discussed in this chapter. Decide what changes need to be made in your grouping.

3. Consider your ministry to the homebound and the institutionalized. What plan should be made for improving this ministry? Perhaps you will want a fully organized home department.

4. Consider each of the trends listed. Work on the implications for your local church.

FOR FURTHER STUDY

Clemmons, Robert S., *Young Adults in the Church,* Nashville: Abingdon Press, 1959, chaps. 4, 5. 138 pp.

Lentz, Richard E., *Making the Adult Class Vital,* St. Louis, Mo.: Bethany Press, 1954, chaps. 3, 7, 8. 112 pp.

Maves, Paul B., *Understanding Ourselves as Adults,* Nashville: Abingdon Press, 1959, chap. 5. 217 pp.

Zeigler, Earl F., *Christian Education of Adults,* Philadelphia: Westminster Press, 1958, chaps. 5, 6. 142 pp.

DO ⋮ **DON'T**

When too many calls compete for our interest, we may lose interest in all of them

5 Strength Through Fellowship

Camping one night on a western mountain slope, we had an unforgettable experience. The wind blew, the rain poured, and the lightning flashed. With every flash we could see tall pine trees bending toward the ground; then in the darkness we could hear one after another break and crash to the ground, crushing everything within its reach. We did not understand why these sturdy trees should fall so easily until we learned that during the winter a logging company had taken out about half of the trees. Left without the support and protection of the grove, trees that had withstood many a harder storm broke and fell crashing to the ground.

Then I thought: This is a parable of man. In the present world of storm and disaster, man needs the support and protection of others. He cannot long endure alone.

The Power to Help Each Other

Adults are looking for a source of strength in a stormy world. They look for a power of being that is equal to the demands, the relationships, and the opportunities of life. Reuel Howe describes as the power of the personal, the "power to hear and to help one another, and, incidentally, to be heard and helped ourselves; the power to live together with mutual helpfulness and creativeness."[1] In our threatened world we are coming to realize how truly adults need each other for strength and growth. Another writer has said, "The human life grows, like other life, through some form of interplay of forces within and the conditions without. But the primary influence in stimulating the growth of persons is that of other persons."[2]

Man lives by and through relationships rather than by rugged individualism. He becomes strong to the extent that he moves out from himself and becomes a participant in an ever-widening world about him. The test of his strength is the interplay of relationships between himself and others.

As we look to the early days of the Christian church, we find dynamic and strength in a costly fellowship. Here we have a few rather unpromising individuals who, inflamed by the sense of a great cause, sold everything, and did not even consider their lives too dear a price for the cause. Trueblood points out that Jesus left his cause in the hands of such a fellowship; he continues to say, "The creation of such a fellowship is the argument that can count in the confused world of our day. . . . If there should emerge in our day such a fellowship, wholly without artificiality and free from the dead hand of the past, it would be an exciting event of momentous importance. A society of loving souls, set free from self-seeking struggle for personal prestige and from all unreality, would be something unutterably precious.[3] The fellowship concept holds that the strength one finds in the group is determined by the quality of his relationships with other persons in the group. Sherrill expresses this idea in these words: "The self is formed in its relationships with others. If it becomes deformed, it becomes so in its relationships. If it is reformed, it becomes so in its relationships."[4]

There is no question here! As the pine tree needs the grove in time of storm, even more man needs the strength of a concerned fellowship—else he may break under the winds of life.

Where Else but the Church?

Where else but through the church can man find this strength? When Jesus set up his church to be the redemptive fellowship, he declared that where groups meet in his name, he is there in reality (Matt. 18:20). But such groups are too few, even in the church. Far too often the church has become an organization or an institution rather than being the "fellowship of the concerned." Groups have become cliques with an "in-group" and a "fringe group." Persons may become lost in the business of making the group large. They may even be exploited or manipulated in order that the church may appear successful. Thousands think of the adult groups of the church as stuffy and formal, concerned mainly with repetition and convention. Often there is much politeness and correctness, but nothing *real* happens. People are too afraid and too selfish to communicate successfully about the deep issues of life; and so they stand alone in the storm, even though they are in the midst of people.

But such a situation need not exist. The church potentially is the accepting, loving, forgiving leaven of society. The best possible method of evangelism is in force when persons within such a fellowship grow in strength and begin to share their experience with others. It is, therefore, within the church that man may hope to find such a fellowship—a fellowship through which each adult can feel himself becoming what God intended him to be.

A Channel for the Holy Spirit

When men give themselves in full and free response to God, the Holy Spirit operates to bring about a fellowship which is indeed redemptive. Man, through feeling himself a part of a forgiving, accepting group, may dare take down the barriers and open his life to the Holy Spirit. Thus, such a group may become an avenue for the entrance of the Holy Spirit. While man knows that he cannot create the redemptive fellowship, he also knows that he has a very important part to play in creating conditions for such a fellowship. Confident that the Holy Spirit will not fail us, we turn to man's part in creating the conditions for this redemptive fellowship.

Building the Fellowship

The whole church, when it is redemptively alive, is such a fellowship as we have been describing. Yet what has been said applies equally well to any group of Christians, for the presence of the Holy Spirit has been promised wherever Christians meet in the name of Christ. Therefore, the promise is for every adult Sunday school class, every adult club of the church, every study group. Such groups can be far more than lecture or discussion periods, teas, or meetings. They may truly become the source of deep change which brings growth and strength.

On being a leader. The relationship of the leader to the group is of utmost importance if the group is to be a dynamic fellowship. The concept the leader has of his role will affect the functioning of the group also.

Take Jim Evans. Jim has an extravertive personality and is well liked. He can get people to do what he wants them to do. He plans his outline for the discussion, and follows his plan. He lets the members of the class discuss projects, but they usually decide his way. He meets with every committee. The class is active with service projects and social meetings. It is a large, "successful" class. Jim has a number of followers who come to the class because he is the leader. People say the class would fall apart if Jim should resign. Jim enjoys the class and gives every spare minute to its success. Is he a good leader? That depends on your concept of leadership. There is no question that Jim leads and others follow. In a way, he is a subtle dictator who enjoys his prestige and success. Perhaps, unconsciously, he is more concerned with the success of the group than with what is really happening to persons in the group. There is no question but that the group is leader centered; and such leadership tends to make the members dependent on the leader. However skillful he may be, does Jim not guide members in the direction of his desires? Thus they become outer-controlled, rather than developing confidence as self-directing, fully responsible persons. His group may be a "success," but it will not be a redemptive fellowship; for, according to this conception of leadership, the responsibility lies on the leader.

Or take Linda Gordon. Linda says that she believes in "permissive" leadership and feels that she has little to do. She introduces the lesson topic, and the members just talk. They discuss projects and social activities, but these never seem to materialize. The group becomes chaotic and frustrated. They are like sheep without a shepherd. Is Linda a "permissive" leader? No, she has abdicated leadership, but she holds the title so that no one else may really become leader.

Then there is Dr. Black. He is a college professor with a major in history. He feels that his chief responsibility is to be an interrogator to ferret out the facts and the main issues. The focus of his attention is on subject matter. Those who attend his sessions say they get a great deal of "content." While Dr. Black's approach may be appropriate if the aim is to gain subject mastery, it has serious limitations in providing strength through fellowship or in effecting changed attitudes or personal growth.

A different approach to leadership is being attempted by Ken Cowper. Ken hopes to help the group take responsibility for its own progress. He holds that leadership should reside in the group and that his job is to assist the group to make its own decisions. Sometimes leadership functions are performed by several or by all the members. At other times Ken must take the initiative in order to help them make progress. He takes the attitude of a fellow searcher whose function is to set a climate for honest learning. He has a feeling of deep respect for the integrity of every person in the group, thus establishing a spirit of free and democratic participation. In speaking of himself Ken says, "I'm not really the teacher of the group. We teach each other. I think of myself more as a convener and stimulator than as a leader. Sure, we discuss material, especially the Bible, but rather than my telling them, we all together try to understand what it says to us today."

Here we have four differing concepts of leadership. Jim Evans is an example of leader-centered leadership. His is the "successful," "go-getter" class without too much regard for persons and how they feel about themselves. Linda Gordon, while she believes herself to be permissive, really practices laissez-faire leadership. She is too passive to be an acceptable leader. Dr. Black is the traditional type of leader. His purpose is to present subject matter, with little consideration of personality change. Ken Cowper is endeavoring to follow a group-centered procedure. He desires to help the individual satisfy his needs through serving the group needs. He practices democratic leadership.

What difference does the leader's concept of his role make? Studies in leadership point up that all aspects of group functioning may better be handled by the group rather than by an individual designated as the leader. Kurt Lewin and his helpers investigated the effects of these different kinds of leaders on various groups. "Democratic leadership, in which the leader helped the group to organize itself and to make its own decisions, proved consistently to produce the best results in terms of things accomplished, co-operative relationships, and personal growth. The groups under authoritarian leadership, in which the leader maintained rigid control, produced less and encountered a great deal more friction and frustration. The groups that scored the lowest on all counts were those under laissez-faire leadership, in which the leader remained completely passive."[5]

While it is seldom that any leader follows in a clear-cut way any one of these types of leadership, each does have his own concept of leadership. If the group is to find strength through fellowship, the leadership must be increasingly group centered.

GROUP LEADERSHIP

Is this the pattern?

1. The leader is active and aggressive; the members are passive. They expect the leader to think up the plans and carry them out or see that they do.

2. The material is the final answer. The students are to know what is there and be able to recite it.

3. Knowledge is objective, and the mature person accepts it without emotion.

4. Discussion is a slow process. Pupils are not authorities on a subject. Their part is confined to listening and asking questions.

5. Keeping to the point and covering the subject is paramount. Problems arising in the class must be handled with dispatch.

6. The leader uses committees to carry out his ideas.

Can it be changed to this?

1. The members are helped to feel their own responsibility. Each is encouraged to make his contribution to the success of the group.

2. The material is source material, to be used in dealing with problems and making decisions.

3. Learning is tied up with emotion. The leader is sensitive to how members feel about the subject, toward him, and toward each other.

4. Persons learn better when they have an opportunity to test their ideas. It takes time and a great deal of "pushing an idea around" before it really becomes a part of one's life.

5. The leader is a guide to see that significant problems are discussed thoroughly.

6. Committees have freedom to carry out a project in their own way.

7. Learning is getting ideas across. The usual pattern is for the leader to present facts, ask questions, comment on each contribution, and summarize the lesson.

7. Learning is growth in understanding and in ability to handle life's problems. Variety in method aids learning. So the leader uses discussion, panels interviews, role-playing, field trips, and other methods.

8. The leader feels that he is responsible for the success or failure of the group.

8. While the leader is willing to do his part, he places large responsibility for the progress of the group on the group itself.

On being a group member. Adults, even in a democracy, have become so accustomed to being outer-controlled that most of them will have to learn how to be a member of a fellowship group. Inherently they hunger for the experience of deep communion and trust, but from life they have learned that there are few persons with whom it is safe to be their real selves. To make all members of the crew and permit no passengers,° as Trueblood has said, means to give up forever the careless go-and-come-as-you-please type of attendance. If the group is to carry responsibility, there must be regular attendance at the functions of the group. One gives up being a spectator who sits passively to be entertained or to have something done to him. Instead, as a member of the crew, he takes responsibility according to his ability and feels a personal stake in the success of the group.

Fellowship group members experience a relationship that reaches far outside the study sessions and continues throughout the week and even through life. (This is the chief reason that the group should remain relatively stable, as was discussed in Chapter 4.) They are friends who visit in each other's homes. They share their joys and their sorrows. They help each other in time of need. They pray for each other. They celebrate victories together. They join together in projects of service and mercy. In fact, they become responsible for one another in a deep and meaningful way. All this may seem rather costly to members who have not learned to invest themselves in others, but such is necessary if man is to feel the power of the group.

But also, adults may have to learn how to be responsible members of the study group. Each will need to develop objectivity in discussion so that he can appreciate, or at least tolerate, conflicts of opinion. He will learn to discipline his own contributions, sticking to the point and allowing others the right to be heard. He will really listen to every person and try to understand exactly what is being said. He will exert initiative in encouraging personal involvement and evoking hard thinking in the group. He will be honest in his expression, rather than saying what he thinks is expected. He will be open in his life to the implications of new truth which dawns on him. Now, no one learns how to be a good group member in a month, or even in a year. Being this kind of member is something like becoming a mature personality—always maturing, but never perfect.

The Maturing Group

Knowles points out that groups seem to go through much the same kind of development as do persons. He says, "During its beginning stage, for example, a group exhibits many of the characteristics of an infant child. It is dependent upon the guiding hand of a parent [the leader]. It seeks his approval. It has difficulty in co-ordinating the efforts of its members. Its goals are likely to be poorly defined."[7] Many adult classes seem to stay in this period of dependency. Such is likely to be true of leader-centered groups led by such persons as Jim Evans. As long as there is strong, active leadership they hold together, with members becoming more and more dependent.

However, the first meetings of any new group are largely taken up with the members testing themselves and each other. They have to learn whether the climate is safe or not. There is likely to be difficulty in communication or verbal misunderstandings. There may be a very polite effort to say the expected, with no real honesty or involvement in the group. These and other infantile patterns seem to appear regardless of the maturity of individual members.

Just as individuals resist change, so groups also resist. It is not unusual for a group to attempt to go back to the traditional pattern after some progress has been made toward the freedom of the more permissive group. Some members express this resistance by withdrawal (either from the discussion, from taking responsibility, or maybe from the whole group). Others insist that the leader show more leadership. Some express a feeling of lostness by such terms as: "Why don't you tell us the answers?" "Just decide and tell us what to do." "We waste too much time in group decisions." The members at this stage will frequently show irritation toward each other, sometimes disagree with the leader, and may even request a change of leaders. If members are absent or fail to express an opinion when decisions are made, they complain that their wishes were not considered.

Knowles calls this the adolescent stage of group development.[8] He says that it is characterized by the struggle between the desire for independence and the fear of leaving the protection of a guiding hand. This is a threatening period to the group, and a skillful and understanding leader is required if the group is to survive. Threatened, the leader may revert to authority ("take over the reins"), and the group congeals into the traditional adult class. Or determined to remain permissive, he may fail to assist the group to understand what is happening, and thus he retards their development. Even worse, he may with a sense of failure abandon the whole project. In this case disintegration will likely set in, for persons having sensed the freedom and value of such an emerging fellowship are not easily satisfied. However, if the leader is wise and helps the group to understand this process of natural growth, the group can use this experience as a means to maturity.

As a group reaches toward maturity, it becomes more able to accept responsibility for its own actions. The members can discuss any subject with honesty and with some measure of objectivity. There are no ideas which have to be "left outside the door" because they cannot be mentioned. The group faces its problems and solves them objectively. It divides its tasks among its members in keeping with their abilities. The members have changed their center of concern from personal goals, such as status, to group goals, such as making decisions that will benefit all. The leader acts as the convener, but the real leadership is a function of the group. They can accept evaluation and self-criticism in such a way as to profit by it. Because the group has thus matured, the climate of learning described in Chapter 2 has become a reality. There will be freedom of expression, responsible participation, a feeling of warmth, and a sense of search.

THE GROUP

Actions of an immature group	*Actions of a maturing group*
1. The atmosphere is stiff and formal. Chairs are in rows. People address each other as Mrs. Jones and Dr. Black. Visitors have formal introductions.	1. The atmosphere is warm and friendly. The room is homelike. Members use first names and seem to like each other.
2. Members are very polite to each other. They seem afraid to disagree with the leader or others.	2. Members are courteous but frank. They can disagree and still be friendly.
3. Members avoid controversial issues for fear of hurt feelings and argument.	3. The group discusses controversial issues with a measure of objectivity.
4. There is much evidence of status-seeking in the group, with some cliques being formed. Members are judged by position, money, clothes, education, or refinement.	4. The group functions as a one-level democratic social system. Each contribution to the group must stand on its own merit.

5. Each person is so busy thinking of his place in the group that he doesn't listen to what others say.

5. Members try to gain real understanding of each other and listen attentively.

6. The group either ignores its silent members or tries to force them to talk.

6. The group tries to use the abilities of all members. The contributions are to be voluntary, and so no one insists that others talk or take responsibility.

7. Decisions are made by vote, and majority rules.

7. The group tries to avoid voting and seeks to reach decisions by consensus.

8. Compromise is regarded as weak and undesirable.

8. Constructive compromise is seen as more desirable than having one side win at the loss of the other side.

9. Opinions are expressed without clarification of the issues involved.

9. Members try to see both sides of an issue before expressing their opinions.

10. The matter of guiding the group is left to the leader who then receives credit for success or blame for failure.

10. Members perform various roles as needed; therefore they share in many leadership functions.

The Functioning Fellowship

The assumptions underlying the formation of fellowship groups are found in man's need to be a dynamic person. These were discussed in some detail in Chapter 1. However, the earlier approach was from the viewpoint of the individual rather than as a function of the group. Here the question is: How does the fellowship function to meet personal needs?

The need to grow in freedom. The maturing fellowship is the very place where man can have a sense of freedom. Since here he feels safe to be his honest self, he does not need to try to make people think he is better or smarter or richer than he really is. He can take off his mask and not only let others know him, but may even see himself as in a mirror and learn what sort of person he really is. In an atmosphere of freedom and mutual acceptance, he is not compelled to conform and so can be honest.

Priscilla David had this very experience. Priscilla was a leader in the church and thought of herself as a model of piety. For the sake of her example she disciplined herself strictly and expected a great deal of her children. When her only daughter became involved with a married man, Priscilla felt broken and disgraced. For righteousness' sake, she rejected her daughter and turned her out. But one day she found herself in a retreat where a fellowship was forming. At first she was stiff and the paragon of goodness, but gradually she saw how unreal she was. Then in a role-playing session, by chance, she experienced the terrors of being rejected. She realized the suffering her attitude had caused both her daughter and herself. She learned that she could accept her daughter without approving the wrong deed. She experienced freedom in relationship to her daughter for the first time in her life. She also experienced a new relationship with others, as through her forgiveness the forgiving love of God filled her life.

The need for a sense of belonging. There is no better way to develop a sense of belonging than through taking responsibility for each other and for the development of the group. This is one reason why all must become involved in the success or failure of the experience. If one would really have the sense of belonging, there can be no dainty gestures of helping. One must put his shoulder to the load and give it all that he has. For many people life is meaningless because they have been unwilling to really give themselves to any person or any cause. A vital Christian fellowship, with all its potential for evangelism and service, can provide a sense of belonging, for its success requires one's best.

The need to become involved with other persons. It is true that each individual is the center of his own private world of experience, and he reacts to reality from this viewpoint. But as he comes into a group where he can understand and accept himself and where he feels others understand and accept him, he lets down his barriers and shows more understanding and acceptance of others. It is only when this happens that he can become involved with others in a meaningful way. Priscilla David, for example, for the first time is close enough to her daughter to really help her. She has accepted her own part of the responsibility for her daughter's problem, and they are learning to love each other on an adult level.

The need to understand life's deeper meanings. The individual comes to understand life's deeper meanings as he experiences the honest, trusting, accepting, and loving atmosphere of the fellowship. Here the body of Christian truth which is the rich heritage of the church can become meaningful in a personal way. In this kind of atmosphere the members will also feel free to bring the realities of life outside the classroom for discussion and evaluation. Real life issues must be discussed, described, and identified within the supporting relationship of the group. Learners must see themselves as being involved in the issues under consideration and judge all by the high standard of the gospel. Thus, the heritage becomes valuable to the learner only as he appropriates it to himself. The methods of teaching most effective for such an experience would of necessity be informal with a great deal of freedom in the curriculum.[9]

The need to co-operate in creativity. In becoming a participating member of a group which he feels to be creative and redemptive, the individual finds a corner where he can get hold to lift his part of the load. If the group is what it may be, he will find creative expression through projects of service and mercy. Here, he can sense the satisfaction of working with others and with God in helping people to the more abundant life.

It would appear that as we look at man's basic needs, we glimpse the possibility of a true fellowship group as one means by which these needs may be satisfied.

A Fellowship Is Forming

In order to see how the principles work in an actual situation, may we turn now to see how one class of young adults is endeavoring to form a fellowship.

The church had good potential for a young adult fellowship. Since there was no class for those newly married, almost all youth had dropped out of Sunday school when they were married. In checking with the church secretary, it was determined that at least fifteen couples were connected with the church more or less loosely, none of whom attended Sunday school. Four couples were attending, but they were unhappy because there was no class for them. An older couple saw the need and offered their services as sponsors in order to try to build a fellowship. The board of Christian education felt the need also. They approved the idea and suggested that the group be limited to those who had been married eight years or less. They furnished a large fellowship room and agreed to assist in buying curriculum materials.

Step 1. The sponsors invited to their home several couples who could be key leaders. Talking with them about trying to develop a group, they found a real need and interest. Three couples agreed to be a sponsoring committee to help get the group started. Each agreed to contact one third of the couples on the secretary's list to tell them about the possibility of the group. The hostess served refreshments at the close of the planning session. (Eating together helps develop fellowship.)

Step 2. The sponsoring committee decided to have an overnight planning retreat to talk over purposes, study materials for organization, and get better acquainted. The retreat was a real success. Nearly all the potential members were present. The program included recreation, food (lots of it), planning meetings, a Christmas exchange, worship, some (?) sleeping, morning watch, and discussion.

Step 3. The group chose the following principles to guide them.

a) They wanted to be a continuing fellowship rather than merely a class. They were willing to begin with those who had been married eight years or less, but they wanted to add one year each year, so that they would have a feeling of permanency.

b) Since they wanted each person to have equal responsibility, they planned to function through a sponsoring committee of three couples. Each couple would serve three months, with a new couple being added each month and one going off. The committee would plan social activities, remember special occasions, plan projects, and look after the progress of the group. The leaders were to have charge of the class discussions and help the group in organizing itself.

c) The group really wanted to know each other, and so they asked for a variety of social occasions. During the first year they had the following social activities: the overnight retreat, a progressive dinner, a bowling party with refreshments at the home of one of the members, an overnight camping trip on the beach, a homemade ice-cream social, an international dinner, and a semiformal banquet for their first birthday.

They drew names to invite each other to their homes. They welcomed each newly married couple with a gift, and also each new baby.

Since they often do not see each other during the week, the group decided to gather early and use the first ten minutes each Sunday for fellowship over coffee, followed by worship, then discussion.

d) They wanted to choose their own subjects for study. They desired freedom of opinion and an opportunity for each to express any honest thought that might contribute to their search for meaning and depth in living the Christian life. When they were ready for a new subject of study, they used some such interest indicator as Chart IV in the appendix of this book. During the first year they studied: *Understanding Myself and Others*,[10] Hogue; *Your God Is Too Small*,[11] Phillips; *The Common Ventures of Life*,[12] Trueblood; The *Talk-back* Television Series.

Step 4. They chose a name. As the group continued to grow, they felt they needed a name by which to be identified. They felt that a name should be symbolic of the experience they were having and that it would help them realize their own unity. The search for a suitable name was long and difficult. They considered such names as Berean, Loyalty, Friendship, Kum-Double, and Yoke-fellows. Finally they settled on "The Questers," and the longer they use it, the better they like it.

Step 5. They wanted to serve. Here is one of the hazards of the group. They want to serve in the church and help the needy. Yet they, themselves, are just becoming organized as a family. They find it difficult to give enough time or money to carry through satisfying projects, yet they must do this if they would become a real fellowship. They have joined with other groups in regular visits to a mental hospital to share with the patients in recreation and worship. They have served the church in caring for the nursery. The church increasingly looks to the group for teachers. At present, eight of the regular church school teachers are from the group and six others are in training for leadership. On a recent Sunday, more than half the members were out teaching or serving in some other way. This led to a proposal of an honor roll of those who take regular responsibility in other classes during the discussion period. They are to drop by the room during the coffee period for a word of greeting and blessing.

Step 6. They decided to evaluate the progress of the group. After a year they should now do some careful evaluating of the progress of the group. Just what has the group meant to each member? How does each member feel about his relationship to the group? What concept of leadership has developed? In what stage of development is the group? Chart II of the appendix might be used for one part of the evaluation. Also they could use a flow chart (see For Group Planning, Chapter 2) and an observer's chart (Chart III, appendix) to understand participation in discussion. Besides this self-evaluation, they may have an outside observer visit the group for an objective evaluation. The honesty with which each person faces his relationship to the group will determine whether or not this group will continue to grow toward becoming a redemptive fellowship.

For Group Planning

1. A real effort should be made to help classes see the possibilities of the fellowship group. Perhaps the ideas of this chapter could be presented to every group in the church, so that each could consider possible changes for more effectiveness. It may be that the use of Chart II of the appendix would seem more valuable here than in connection with Chapter 1.

2. A study should be made of each age group of the church to see if there is need for forming new groups such as The Questers.

3. In order for the study group to have an experience with various types of leaders and groups, they could participate in a role play of the leaders and their groups as described in this chapter, in the section on "Being a leader." First, they would choose someone to role play Jim Evans, and have the group respond as they feel would be natural; likewise someone would play Linda Gordon, and the others. This could make a good introduction to a discussion on the concept of leadership.

4. The church should make provision for its leaders to attend workshops where the principles discussed in this chapter are in operation.

FOR FURTHER STUDY

Caldwell, Irene S., *Adults Learn and Like It*, Anderson, Ind.: Warner Press, 1955, chaps. 2, 3. 112 pp.

Cantor, Nathaniel, *The Dynamics of Learning*, New York: George W. Stewart, Publisher, Inc., 1946, chaps. 5, 6, 7, 11, 12, 13, 14, 15.

Clemmons, Robert S., *Dynamics of Christian Adult Education*, Nashville: Abingdon Press, 1958, chaps. 7, 9. 143 pp.

———, *Young Adults in the Church*, Nashville: Abingdon Press, 1959, chap. 3. 138 pp.

Howe, Reuel L., *The Creative Years*, Greenwich, Conn.: The Seabury Press, 1958, chap. 2. 239 pp.

Knowles, Malcolm S., *Informal Adult Education*, New York: Association Press, 1950, chap. 4. 272 pp.

Little, Sara, *Learning Together in the Christian Fellowship*, Richmond, Va.: John Knox Press, 1956, chaps. 1, 4. 104 pp.

Ross, Murray G. and Hendry, Charles E., *New Understandings of Leadership*, New York: Association Press, 1957. 158 pp.

Sherrill, Lewis J., *The Gift of Power*, New York: The Macmillan Company, 1955, chaps. 2, 3, 4. 202 pp.

Trueblood, Elton, *Alternative to Futility*, New York: Harper and Brothers, 1948, chaps. 3, 4, 5. 124 pp.

———

[1]Reuel Howe, *The Creative Years*, The Seabury Press, Greenwich, Conn., p. 21. Used by permission.

[2]John W. Schackford, *Education in the Christian Religion*, Cokesbury Press, 1931, p. 119. Used by permission.

[3]Elton Trueblood, *Alternative to Futility*, Harper and Brothers, p. 34.

[4]Lewis J. Sherrill, *The Gift of Power*, The Macmillan Company, 1955, p. 45.

[5]Malcolm S. Knowles, *Informal Adult Education*, Association Press, 1950, p. 60.

[6]Trueblood, *op. cit.*, p. 74.

[7]Knowles, *op. cit.*, p. 55.

[8]*Ibid.*, p. 56.

[9]A rather detailed discussion of teaching techniques suitable for such a group is given in *Adults Learn and Like It*, Irene S. Caldwell, Warner Press, 1955.

[10]Helen G. Hogue, *Understanding Myself and Others*, The Abingdon-Cokesbury Press, 47 pages.

[11]J. B. Phillips, *Your God Is Too Small*, The Macmillan Company, 140 pages.

[12]Elton Trueblood, *The Common Ventures of Life*, Harper and Brothers, 124 pages.

Real living is filled with curiosity for new discoveries

6 Outlets for Creative Power

The Creative Power Within

Every adult has within him a great wealth of creative ability. It is one of the most valuable gifts he possesses. This is the force within him that will not let him accept happily the routine and the ordinary. It is the power that drives him to invent new machines and explore new planets, write poetry and create masterpieces. It makes him want to improve conditions and provide a richer way of life for people everywhere. It sends him into dangerous places to take the message of life and salvation. The source of this creative power is God, who in his infinite love has given to each man a part of his own greatness—the power to create—so that each may build a worth-while way of life.

But man is so concerned with being really alive and so afraid of having lived in vain, that this very fear may destroy his creativity. Either he may give up the struggle and settle into his dull little rut, or he may sap his creativity by restless straining against his limitations. If adults can learn how to use their creative powers, their lives will be tremendously fruitful. Here is the real teaching task of the adult church school. To challenge adults to be alive and creative and to provide outlets for this creative power is an opportunity beyond description. As a channel for the power of God, the church may provide the strength whereby adults become able to meet the crises of life with joyful faith, to obtain courage to break routine patterns of thought and action, and to move into creative experimentation.

Outlets for Creative Power

Learning to use this creative power is the secret of growing, satisfying adulthood. When man comes to understand himself as an instrument of the creativity of God, his life becomes significant and challenging. With this attitude his job is no longer a matter of necessary evil or dull routine. It becomes instead a means of co-operation in the eternal task. His recreation becomes another opportunity for self-expression. His friendships become an excursion in sharing and mutual growth. He feels himself in tune with God in every aspect of creativity. He lives a full and exciting life. Such is God's plan for every adult.

We see this creative power at work in the lives of children. Each child finds life a great exploration. He is incurably curious and is excited about each new discovery, whether it be the mystery of a seed which grows or a plant which blooms. Youth, although sometimes cynical, nevertheless look forward to life with hope. They feel that life offers great opportunity for them. But adults, in the effort to adjust the dream to the reality, often lose the dream entirely and settle for making a mere living and a nightly session before the television set. This marks the death of creativity.

Maintaining the creative attitude in a success-conscious world presents one of the hardest struggles of adulthood. Creativity accepts tension and struggle as necessary to life. The creative person resists every effort of his job, or even of his church, to take away his originality and fit him into its mold. But at the same time he realizes his need to be a responsible member of a group. He needs their belief in him, their challenge, their love, and the feeling that they need him. How can the adult fellowship of the church help its members in their struggle to keep creativity alive? What are the main outlets for creative power?

Creative thought. The spirit of the thought life of the church must be one of honest search. This idea has been called "faith with your eyes wide open." The growing Christian develops a firm faith on which he stakes his life. He holds certain things to be true, but he is still searching for deeper and more significant interpretations. He realizes that truth has never been fully explored, and he wants to assume his part in the exploration. The very climate of the group can be such as to stifle creative thought, or it can encourage it. When persons in the church start thinking creatively, things happen. They find powers and satisfactions which they did not know were possible. Laying aside authoritarianism in doctrine and formality in practice, the church may encourage adults to find power through creative thought, under the guidance of the Holy Spirit.

Creative work. Since the beginning of time men and women have spent a large percentage of each day in work. Man's feeling about his work can make a great difference, no matter what the work may be. Man needs to examine his motive for working. If he is working for the wrong reason, he can never expect creative results. If man works for pay only, even though the pay may be used for a worth-while purpose, the quality of service will be only good enough to obtain the pay. Such a motive does not encourage the creative experiences of life. The same is true of working for the sake of status. Since the motive is selfish, man is sorely tempted to manipulate others for his own success. Such a relationship is bound to alienate others and thus stifle creative relationships.

If man can see his work as a part of God's work his work need not be a routine burden; rather it will be a source of great happiness because it is his way of making a contribution to his world. To the garment maker who "goes through the motions," the factory can become a prison and the machine an enemy. But if he can see himself as helping God to clothe the world warmly and beautifully, he can take pride in the contribution. He will look for ways of cutting down waste and making a better garment. He can go home with the satisfaction in his heart of doing his part to make the world a better place.

The adult church school can help people have a creative attitude toward work by lifting all worthy and needed work to the level of vocation. Each person must feel, "The circumstances being what they are, this is God's way for me to serve at present. Therefore I will do my work joyfully and as a service to God." No experience of a Christian is to be seen as apart from the will of God.

Underlying this philosophy of work is the teaching that all of life is sacred and is to be lived in harmony with the will of God. God is just as much worshiped in a piece of work done to his glory as in a service of worship. In fact, one is dependent on the other. Trueblood points up this idea by saying, "We must see our religion, not primarily as what goes on in a peculiar building with pointed arches and stained glass windows, but as the way in which all ordinary enterprises are conducted."[1] Again he says, "That religion will have most meaning which touches common life redemptively at the most points."[2] If the church can help each person feel that his work is a sacred privilege and opportunity to serve, a blessing instead of a curse, then the church has opened up a powerful outlet for creative energy.

This is not to say that all work is of equal value as a worship to God and in service to fellow men. Some work is not suitable for Christians because it is essentially harmful or parasitical rather than producing goods or services really needed. Other work is not suited to the capacity of the worker. Each person must be realistic; but under a sense of divine calling he is to find the work open to him which will be most productive in eternal values. Adults sorely need guidance in finding creative outlets through work. They should be able to look to the church for such help.

Creative play. Another outlet for creative ability is play. This is an important part of life for grownups as well as for children. Creative play means using free time for self-expression. Recreation is a good word to use in describing this experience, for it has great power as a source of creativity. Yet this new free time has been greatly exploited for economic profit with devastating social and spiritual ills.

Listening to music is fine if one really listens and gives himself to the harmony and beauty; but playing music is better; and creating music may be best of all. The music created may not be great, but the pleasure in it is great because it is the expression of the inner feelings of the person himself. The same is true of sports, writing, art, or handcrafts. The finished product may not be perfect, but it is firsthand, and it becomes a means for self-expression.

In recreation, the adult church school again has an opportunity to provide a creative outlet. This task may be difficult, for many adults have settled for an occasional dinner out and some sort of vicarious experience rather than for participation. Even the church has succumbed almost entirely to the recreation of eating and listening, especially for adults. But if the church will develop a Christian basis for its recreation and offer a variety of opportunities, adults will respond, perhaps timidly at first, but later in a wholehearted way. Some of the qualities of creative recreation are given below.

Recreation is likely to be creative if:

1. It provides for a maximum of participation.
2. It is genuinely interesting.
3. It is fun and can be continued through life.
4. It provides the opportunity for individuality.
5. It is thought provoking.
6. It releases physical energy and emotions.
7. It provides opportunity for human associations and recognition.
8. It provides for self-expression and balance.
9. It opens a variety of new interests.
10. It leads to social sensitiveness and co-operation.

In order to meet these qualities the church would provide or at least stimulate interest in four types of recreation.

There is need for *physical recreation*. While some limitations will need to be considered here with advancing adulthood, there is evidence that all ages of adults enjoy all the recreational activities suited to younger groups.

There is need for *manual recreation*. This applies primarily to handcrafts, but reaches out to include hobbies as well. While this type recreation is pursued alone, recognition is gained through shows and exhibits. Thus it provides opportunity for individuality, but it is social as well.

There is also need for *social recreation*. This is the type provided through picnics, parties, and dinners. Here there is stimulating conversation, laughter, and fun. Both men and women need regularly to put on their best clothes and their best manners and forget themselves in sharing their sharpest wit and most interesting ideas. Such "occasions" can call forth a great deal of creativity.

And there is need for *cultural recreation,* including drama, music, reading, travel, art, and crafts. As man grows, so should his cultural interests and appreciations. Walter Russell Bowie has said, "We live according to the number, depth, and richness of our interests. That man lives most who responds with enthusiasm and joy to most of the fine things about him: books, music, art, drama, a lovely sunset, a flower garden, a trip through the woods, a quiet period of worship, a chance to serve, the fellowship of a friendly game, the opportunity to converse with friends, the thrill of a creative hobby, the song of a robin, and a thousand other joys."[3]

Creative helpfulness. Here is a challenge to the greatest power within man! It asks that men learn how to help one another along the way of life. Too often the spirit of adulthood has been that of "live and let live" rather than "live and help live." In man there seems to be the need to compete with others, rather than a desire to help them. But competition undercuts co-operation and ends in anxiety and strife. If man can feel within himself a sincere desire to be helpful, he has opened a floodgate of creative power.

Consider how the helpful attitude affects friendship. A friendship can be a dull, time-passing experience, or it may be an exciting experience of growing and sharing. Which it is depends on whether the purpose of the friendship is to receive or to give. If the purpose on the part of either is primarily to receive, the experience will be shallow and empty. When in a real friendship each shares of what he is with the other, the result is infinitely rich and creative.

Or consider the love relationship. This is probably the greatest single outlet for creativity. The love of husband and wife, or parent and child, can become a wholehearted and joyful giving of one's self in order to build a life together. As long as the relationship is built on a spirit of helpfulness and true concern, each for the other, love flourishes; but let self-seeking and a spirit of competition enter, and love withers and dies on the vine.

The attitude of helpfulness calls for the greatest maturity. Only those who have grown from self-love to selfless love have the capacity to give of themselves in helpfulness—to really love others. Herein the adult church school has the highest resource in the divine example of Jesus and in his commandment that man love his neighbor as himself. If, somehow, the church can help man find the will and power to live in the spirit of this commandment, what floodgates of creative power would open!

Creative worship. For the Christian, everything centers in God: the earth, knowledge, work, purpose, and power. Man can grow strong through the power that is in God if he can realize this power through his worship life. He becomes truly creative only as he allows God to move mightily through him. Clarice Bowman has said, "Always when the worship of the living God is made central, it has fired people with moral earnestness, inflamed their ethical zeal, and sent them forth to right wrongs in society. The two cannot be separated—the vertical dimension of man's relationship to God, the horizontal dimension of his relationship with his fellow men."[4] This means that the Christian must look beyond the familiar words and form of worship to seek a deeper understanding of God and of the meaning of life. As he begins to relate his worship to day-by-day living, he will find new challenges to a higher quality of relationships and to becoming a better person. As the church leads adults to worship "in spirit and in truth" it provides outlets of power.

Power Through Commitment

"The meaning of life opens to the person who can give himself to it; to the person who is able to commit himself to his wife, to his children, to his friends, to his work, to his responsibilities, to God. The life of commitment begins with the act of self-giving and is continued by decisions and actions that express that self-giving over and over again."[5] Such an experience culminates in a confrontation of the individual by God as his Lord and Savior, and results in the decision of the whole self in surrender and self-dedication.

Within the fellowship of the church, or some group of the church, man is most likely to have this experience of meeting God and his truth. In fact, it is the purpose of the church to provide the climate for confrontation and decision. Within the community of relationships God confronts the individual at every point of decision. If man refuses to respond to the truth which comes to him, his life becomes arid and dull; but if he answers positively and commits himself wholeheartedly, he feels a release of spiritual power within him. Thus he becomes a channel for God's creative love to flow to others.

The challenging task of the adult church school is to lay aside form and routine and become a living redemptive fellowship. By God's grace and within such a fellowship, adults may find the power to meet every period of life with faith, and thus become growing, dynamic persons.

For Group Planning

1. In the final session of this evaluation, the group will need to test the spirit of the adults in the church. Such testing does not lend itself to charts. Rather, in a spirit of humility let the group ask such questions as the following: Do adults find a challenge to adventurous growth through our groups? Does the church foster honest search for truth? Do adults dare express their honest doubts and criticisms of the church's interpretation of some doctrines? What effort has the church made to help people see religion as related to every experience in life? Does the church clearly give the "vocational" concept of work? How?

What is the church's philosophy of recreation? How does the church develop in its members the attitude of helpfulness?

2. Let the group make a careful check on the program of recreation provided by the church. Chart VI in the appendix may be used for this evaluation. A committee should be authorized to propose a satisfactory program, using the criteria for creative recreation given in this chapter.

3. With heart-searching honesty, let the group consider the challenge to commitment in the church. Does the adult church find real meaning in worship? Is God central? Do members go forth with moral earnestness and ethical zeal? Is the spirit such that persons find themselves confronted by God's righteousness at points of decision? Such an experience should lead the group to an honest facing of the depth of their own commitment.

4. Let the group plan an informal worship service of commitment.

FOR FURTHER STUDY

Bowman, Clarice, *Restoring Worship*, Nashville: Abingdon Press, 1951. 223 pp.

Clemens, Frances; Tully, Robert; Crill, Edward, *Recreation and the Local Church*, Elgin, Ill.: Brethren Publishing House, 1956. 191 pp.

Clemmons, Robert S., *Dynamics of Christian Adult Education*, Nashville: Abingdon Press, 1958. 143 pp.

Howe, Reuel L., *The Creative Years*, Greenwich, Conn.; The Seabury Press, 1958, chaps. 3, 4, 8, 9, 10. 239 pp.

Maves, Paul B., *Understanding Ourselves as Adults*, Nashville: Abingdon Press, 1959, chap. 9. 216 pp.

Sherrill, Lewis J., *The Struggle of the Soul*, New York: The Macmillan Company, 1952, chaps. 7, 8, 9. 155 pp.

Trueblood, Elton, *Alternative to Futility*, New York: Harper and Brothers, 1948, chaps. 3 and 4. 124 pp.

Trueblood, Elton, *The Common Ventures of Life*, New York: Harper and Brothers, 1949, chaps. 1, 4. 124 pp.

[1]Elton Trueblood, *The Common Ventures of Life*, Harper and Brothers, 1949, p. 20.
[2]*Ibid.*, p. 21.
[3]Walter Russell Bowie, *Being Alive*, Scribners.
[4]Clarice Bowman, *Restoring Worship*, Abingdon-Cokesbury Press, 1951, p. 48. Used by permission.
[5]Reuel L. Howe, *The Creative Years*, The Seabury Press, Greenwich, Conn., 1959, p. 214. Used by permission.

Appendix

CHART I. PRESENT ADULT ORGANIZATIONS

(Please attach a list of members.)

NAME OF ORGANIZATION ....

RESPONSIBLE TO WHICH BOARD? ....

PURPOSE ....

FOR WHOM IS PROGRAM PLANNED? ....

MEMBERSHIP: Number of members ....
      Ages .... How enlisted? ....

TYPE OF STUDY MATERIAL ....

TYPE OF PROGRAM ....

HOW IS PROGRAM FINANCED? ....

LEADERS AND OFFICERS ....

CHART II. HOW I FEEL ABOUT THIS GROUP

Name of Group _____

(Each person is to answer with Yes, No, or Sometimes.
He may also add comments.)

Group Climate

The atmosphere is stiff and formal. _____

People are very polite. _____

People are afraid to contribute honestly. _____

The atmosphere is uncertain. _____

People are competitive and argumentative. _____

Members are frank and can disagree pleasantly. _____

The atmosphere is friendly and permissive. _____

There is wide participation. _____

Comments: _____

_____

Sense of Belonging

I feel a very important part of the group. _____

I like the group, but do not feel very important to it. _____

I feel rejected by the group. _____

I would be missed greatly if I dropped out. _____

Others are more important to the group than I am. _____

The group means a great deal to me. _____

Comments: _____

_____

Concern for Each Other

The group shares joys and sorrows. _____

The members of the group choose each other socially. _____

The members turn to each other in time of need. _____

There are a number of close friendships in the group. _____

Comments: _____

_____

Quality of Discussion Materials

   The material is interesting and stimulating. ....

   The material relates to my problems. ....

   I often receive new insights. ....

   I had a part in selecting the material. ....

   We talk, but never get anywhere. ....

   There is little new or challenging. ....

   Comments: ....

....

Opportunity for Service

   The group centers in itself. ....

   We really serve others. ....

   Through the group I find a way to serve. ....

   We plan ways to carry out the ideas we study. ....

   Comments: ....

....

My General Feelings About the Group

....

....

CHART III. OBSERVER'S SHEET

	GAVE INFORMATION	GAVE IDEA	SOUGHT CLARIFICATION	ASKED QUESTION	AGREED	DISAGREED	ARGUED	HELPED ANOTHER
Mr. Jones teacher	XX	XX		X			X	X
Mary Black					X			
Ted James				X		X	X	
Vera Martin		X	X		X			
Don Wilson								
Jim Neff	X	X		X	X			X

CHART IV. INTEREST INDICATOR
IDEAS TO EXPLORE IN OUR GROUP

What ideas do you wish to explore during the coming year?
What are your first, second, third choices?

IDEAS TO EXPLORE	1 ST CHOICE	2 ND CHOICE	3 RD CHOICE	BY WHICH GROUP SHOULD SUBJECT BE STUDIED?
Developing a Mature Faith				
Understanding My Emotions				
Building a Christian Home				
Enriching My Prayer Life				
Being a Christian Steward				
My Daily Witness for Christ				
Missions and the Church				
The Prophets' Message				
Paul's Work and Teachings				
A Christian and His Community				
The Christian and World Conflict				
Making My Vocation Christian				
Christian Use of Leisure Time				
Great Christian Beliefs				
Name other topics of interest to you				

Your name _____

CHART V. CHART ON BALANCED PROGRAM

TYPE OF ACTIVITY NEEDED	YOUNG ADULT	MIDDLE ADULT	OLDER ADULT
Worship			
Study			
Fellowship			
Recreation			
Service			
Evangelism			

(Each type of activity will be considered and rated poor, fair, good, or excellent, according to how well you feel your church is meeting the need of each group.) This chart is to be used in connection with Chapter 2 for a study of six elements in a comprehensive program.

CHART VI. TYPES OF RECREATION

Type	Young Adults	Middle Adults	Older Adults
Physical recreation, such as games and exercises			
Manual recreation, such as handcrafts and hobbies			
Social recreation, such as picnics, parties, dinners			
Cultural recreation, such as art, drama, music, nature, travel, reading			

In each blank indicate ways in which the church has met this need during the past year.